About the author

'Amin's global intellectual reach enables him to deal with a wide variety of issues with magnificent ease and simplicity.'

International Journal of Middle East Studies

'This world-class economist is a serious Nobel Prize contender.'

Economic Development and Social Change

Samir Amin has a reputation as one of the world's foremost radical thinkers. Among his many institutional roles, he has been Director of IDEP (the United Nations African Institute for Planning) from 1970 to 1980; Director of the Third World Forum in Dakar, Senegal; and a co-founder of the World Forum for Alternatives. His works published by Zed Books in English include:

Eurocentrism (1989)
Capitalism in the Age of Globalization: The Management of Contemporary Society (1997)
Obsolescent Capitalism: Contemporary Politics and Global Disorder (2003)
Europe and the Arab World: Patterns and Prospects for the New Relationship, with Ali El Kenz (2005)

Beyond US Hegemony?

Assessing the Prospects for a Multipolar World

———————

SAMIR AMIN

Translated by Patrick Camiller

World Book Publishing
Beirut

SIRD
Kuala Lumpur

UKZN Press
South Africa

ZED BOOKS
London & New York

Beyond US Hegemony? Assessing the Prospects for a Multipolar World
was first published in 2006 by

In Lebanon, Bahrain, Egypt, Jordan, Kuwait, Qatar, Saudi Arabia
and United Arab Emirates: World Book Publishing, Emile Eddeh Street,
Ben Salem bldg, PO Box 3176, Beirut, Lebanon
www.wbpbooks.com

In Malaysia: Strategic Information Research Development (SIRD),
No. 11/4E, Petaling Jaya, 46200 Selangor

In South Africa, Lesotho, Swaziland, Botswana, Namibia and Zimbabwe: University
of KwaZulu-Natal Press, Private Bag XOI, Scottsville 3209, email: books@ukzn.ac.za

In the rest of the world: Zed Books Ltd, 7 Cynthia Street, London N1 9JF, UK,
and Room 400, 175 Fifth Avenue, New York, NY 10010, USA
www.zedbooks.co.uk

Designed and typeset in Monotype Jansen
by illuminati, Grosmont, www.illuminatibooks.co.uk
Cover designed by Andrew Corbett

A catalogue record for this book is available from the British Library
Library of Congress Cataloging-in-Publication Data available
Canadian CIP data is available from the National Library of Canada

ISBN 9953 14 081 2 pb (World Book Publishing)
ISBN 983 2535 77 8 pb (SIRD)
ISBN 1 86914 083 4 pb (University of KwaZulu-Natal Press)
ISBN 1 84277 708 4 hb (Zed Books)
ISBN 1 84277 709 2 pb (Zed Books)
ISBN 978 1 84277 708 4 hb (Zed Books)
ISBN 978 1 84277 709 1 pb (Zed Books)

Contents

Introduction   1

Being clear about the nature of capitalism and imperialism   2
Is there a desirable form of globalization?   5

1   The triad: America, Europe and Japan
    – united or fragmented?   8

The project of the American ruling class: extension of the
    Monroe doctrine to the rest of the world   9
The shifting sands of the European project   14
The clash of political cultures   17
And Japan?   22

2   Does the rise of China challenge the imperialist order?   25

China's rise: revolution or opening to the world?   25
Market socialism: transition, or short-cut to capitalism?   28
So, what is to be done?   39
An uncertain future   46

3   Russia out of the tunnel?   49

Basic characteristics of the Soviet system   50
New forms of capitalism in Russia   54
Is there a worthwhile alternative in Russia today?   64

4   India, a great power?   69

The colonial inheritance   69
Success and limitations of the populist national project   72

The liberal and culturalist drift 77
The long and difficult march of alternative globalization 79

5 Can solidarity be rebuilt among the countries of the South? 84

A critical balance sheet of the 'Bandung era', 1955–75 85
The roots of Africa's exclusion 92
Is South Africa the weak link in the system? 95
Can the slide of the Arab world be reversed? 98
Latin America and the Caribbean in a tricontinental perspective 103
The East as a new South? 105
A new basis for solidarity among the peoples of the South 106

6 Reform of the UN as a part of multipolar globalization 112

Managing national sovereignty within the UN framework 112
A balance sheet of UN activity between 1945 and 1980 115
Conflict and overlap between economic and political management 119
The empire of chaos: sovereignty, social justice and development go by the board 121
The alternative: constructing social justice, international justice and a new popular sovereignty 126
Proposals for a renaissance of the UN 131
A plan for action 144

7 Conclusions 146

The difficulties of constructing a multipolar world 146
Can Washington's military project be thwarted? 148
Thinking long-term 151
Four conditions to be satisfied 157
The great strength of the global 'movement' 160

APPENDIX I Multipolarity in the twentieth century 165

The drama of the great revolutions 166
The weight of imperialism, the permanent stage of the global expansion of capitalism 167
Defence of the post-revolutionary states central to the vanguard's strategic choices 168
Nation-building and/or socialist construction in the radical countries of the periphery 170
Opening debate on the long transition to world socialism 172

APPENDIX II Further reading 175

Index 185

Introduction

The title chosen for the French edition of this book, *Pour un monde multipolaire*, should already be indicative of the author's political position. Yes, I do want to see the construction of a multipolar world, and that obviously means the defeat of Washington's hegemonist project for military control of the planet. In my eyes it is an overweening project, criminal by its very nature, which is drawing the world into wars without end and stifling all hope of social and democratic advance, not only in the countries of the South but also, to a seemingly lesser degree, in those of the North. In this connection, I wrote as long ago as 1991 of the emergence of an 'empire of chaos'.

The term 'multipolar world' calls for some clarification. Like other widely used expressions in the realm of politics, it remains unclear unless and until it is given a precise meaning. For my own part, it implies a recognition that the social system in which we live is thoroughly 'global' or 'globalized', and that any alternative to globalization based on the principles of liberal capitalism (or its more extreme 'neoliberal' form) can itself be nothing other than 'global'. In other words, I am a champion of what has been called 'alter-globalization', not an advocate of 'anti-globalization' in the sense of opposition to any form of globalization. That seems to me not only unrealistic but undesirable.

Disagreements therefore centre on what is meant by multipolarity. Some think of it as a means of 'restoring balance' in the Atlantic alliance, or of ensuring that the other two partners in the triad (the European

Union, or its major powers, and Japan) have a position equal to that of the United States in the running of world affairs. Others go further and argue that there is a need for large countries such as China, Russia, India and Brazil, perhaps even some more or less 'emerging' countries in the South, to have a place in the concert of the major powers.

So far as I am concerned, this is a quite inadequate conception of multipolarity: it does not hold out a satisfactory answer to the real challenges facing the peoples of the world, nor the prospect of social progress that can alone provide a reliable and robust basis for democratization. In other words, my idea of the multipolarity that is necessary today entails a radical revision of 'North–South relations', in all their dimensions. This revision must create a framework that makes it possible to reduce the power of forces within the system (the capitalist system, to call it by its name) that operate in such a way as to exacerbate the polarization of wealth and power. By calling into question the 'imperialist' tradition, or whatever one likes to call it, which governs core–periphery relations in the actually existing capitalist system (something quite different from the general market system dreamed up by mainstream economists), such a revision would automatically pose a challenge to the most fundamental aspects of capitalism. But I should immediately make it clear that, beyond differences of analysis concerning the nature of the system and what appears to be possible or desirable, my argument is intended to open a political debate with all who refuse to align themselves with the unilateralist project of US hegemonism.

Being clear about the nature of capitalism and imperialism

The conception of capitalism as a global system, more than and different from a mere juxtaposition of societies at various stages of capitalist transformation, is not a new idea of mine. The first book I wrote, in 1954–55, already bore the title *Accumulation on a World Scale*, and since then a global vision has been central to my analyses and proposed goals of struggles to 'change the world'. This is not the place to go back over what I have written on these questions. I shall therefore summarize my conclusions by simply recalling that I identify four main phases in the modern globalization associated with capitalist expansion. The first two I call (1) the *mercantilist* phase (1500–1800), during which Atlantic Europe established the core–periphery system through the conquest and reshaping of the Americas, the development of the slave trade and early commercial assaults on Asia (and, to a lesser degree, Africa), and (2) the *classical* phase (1800–1950) of the system, based on a division between industrialized cores and non-industrialized peripheries and a related tendency to reduce the latter to a colonial or semi-colonial status. In (3) the *post-war* phase (1950–1980), the victory of national liberation movements and/or socialist revolutions (which I interpret as radical forms of national liberation) enabled the peripheries to impose a revision of the old asymmetrical terms of the global system and to enter the industrial age. This period of 'negotiated' globalization was exceptional, and it is interesting to note that the world then experienced growth that was the strongest known in history, as well as the least uneven in terms of the distribution of what was produced. In today's *new phase* (4), a global system is being constructed in which the cores (the triad) benefit from 'five monopolies' (more about these later) that give them control over reproduction of the system.

The modern global system of actually existing capitalism has always been polarizing by nature, through the very operation of what I call the 'globalized law of value', as distinct from the law of value *tout court*. In my analysis, therefore, polarization and imperialism are synonymous. I am not among those who reserve the term 'imperialist' for types of political behaviour designed to subjugate one nation to another – behaviour that can be found through the successive ages of the human story, associated with various modes of production and social organization. My analytic interest is anyway geared only to the imperialism of modern times, the product of the immanent logic of capitalist expansion.

In this sense, imperialism is not a stage of capitalism but the permanent feature of its global expansion, which since its earliest beginnings has always produced a polarization of wealth and power in favour of the core countries. The 'monopolies' enjoyed by the cores in their asymmetrical relations with the peripheries of the system define each of the successive phases in the history of the globalized imperialist system.

From the Industrial Revolution (early nineteenth century) to the decades following the Second World War, the monopoly in question was an industrial monopoly; core and periphery were then synonymous with industrialized and non-industrialized countries. We can understand why national liberation movements in the periphery made industrialization their priority, within a wider perspective of 'catching up'. Their success forced imperialism to adapt to this demand. This does not mean that they actually took the road of 'catching up', nor that we entered a 'post-imperialist' period of history. For the core countries then reorganized around new monopolies, which gave them control over technologies and access to the world's natural resources, over international financial flows, communications and the production of weapons of mass destruction. These monopolies cannot fail to reproduce and deepen polarization on a world scale.

Imperialism, from its sixteenth-century origins to the Second World War, was a plural phenomenon; permanent, often violent, conflict between different imperialisms played an important role in shaping the world. In this respect, the Second World War ended with a major transformation, since a collective imperialism of the 'triad' (USA, Europe, Japan) then replaced the multiplicity of imperialisms.

I would suggest that the formation of a new collective imperialism originated in the transformation of competitive conditions. Whereas a few decades ago the large corporations still waged their competitive battles essentially on national markets, the market size now required for victory in the first round of matches is approaching 500 to 600 million 'potential consumers'. The battle therefore has to be fought out directly on the world market, and those who win there can subsequently assert themselves in their own home patch as well. A deeper globalization thus becomes the primary framework for the activity of large corporations. Or, to put it in another way, the causality has been reversed in the national/global couplet: national strength used to control global presence, but today the opposite is the case. Transnational corporations, whatever their country of origin, therefore have common interests in running the world market. These interests overlap with the constant mercantile conflicts that define all the forms of competition peculiar to capitalism.

The dominant segments of transnational capital in all the partners of the triad have a real solidarity with one another that is expressed in their rallying to globalized neoliberalism. The United States is seen as the defender (if necessary the military defender) of these common interests.

But Washington has no intention of sharing 'equitably' the profits of its leadership. On the contrary, it seeks to reduce its allies within the triad to the status of vassals, and is unwilling to allow them more than minor concessions. Is this clash of interests within dominant capital likely to become so pronounced that it leads to a break in the Atlantic alliance?

The conception of globalization that I defend below is one of real and complete multipolarity, in the sense that it gives a place to all nations on earth and concerns 100 per cent of humanity. It contrasts with the truncated multipolarity of all those who implicitly, if not always explicitly, think first of the core triad countries (15 per cent of humanity) and only afterwards grant a few concessions at most to the other 85 per cent. I have always rejected that systematic distortion bound up with the West-centrism of the dominant culture.

Is there a desirable form of globalization?

Since modern globalization and capitalism are inseparable, the globalization that one regards as 'desirable' (unipolar, hierarchically multipolar, non-hierarchically multipolar) will depend on whether one's preferred model of society is liberal capitalism, a more 'social' form of capitalism, or one or another form of socialism. Any option in favour of 'normal' (essentially liberal) capitalism implies an imperialist posture in North–South relations, in accordance with the immanent logic of capital accumulation. At the other end of the spectrum, I would place a radically anti-imperialist approach that recognizes the need to correct the huge North–South inequality in the conditions of production created by five centuries of capitalist expansion. Such a correction evidently implies a socialist perspective (one that goes beyond the basic logic of capital accumulation), but it also requires a conception of global socialism not necessarily shared either by earlier historical socialisms (communist and social-democratic) or by all the currents of new social, and even socialist, thinking.

In what follows, an attempt will always be made to draw out the relationship between proposals for an alternative globalization and certain conceptions of society. The analyses in this work are 'geopolitical', but I should stress that they are in no way inspired by the methods of conventional geopolitics. That discipline, which originated in the nation-alist ruling-class thought of the imperialist countries, treats nation-states as homogeneous invariables, with 'interests' dictated by their geographical location and economic ambitions usually identified with those of the dominant sections of capital. These are the limitations of otherwise excellent works of mainstream geopolitics, such as Paul Kennedy's *The Rise and Fall of the Great Powers.*

My own approach starts from the observation that all countries, in both core and periphery, are beset with social contradictions, and that visions of the society and its place in the international order are not unified at a supposedly national level. Even when a semblance of consensus appears to align the popular classes with their government, rulers and ruled do not necessarily have the same perception of internal or external challenges and of the responses that need to be made to them. I therefore place the emphasis on the contradictions, since only this will allow us to gauge the likelihood of the various conceivable 'scenarios', and to spell out the difficult but possible options that I would like to see strengthened. My analyses will seek to take into account the viewpoints of what are called the social movements (especially the 'alter-globalization' movement), as well as the proposals they explicitly or implicitly put forward.

Without simplifying too much, I would say that the hegemonic blocs in the core countries, which are structured around the dominant seg-ments of capital (especially transnational finance), have an economically 'liberal' and imperialist conception of North–South relations. Conflicts between the state powers in the core take place within this narrowly defined framework – for example, conflicts over whether they should line up with the strategies of US hegemonism or try to limit or even escape their effects. But other hegemonic blocs are possible (particularly in Europe), and we need to examine the conditions under which they might emerge and the range of alternatives they might advance. Such alternative blocs will not necessarily be called upon to make a radi-cal break with the requirements of capitalism, but they may very well force capitalism to adapt to certain demands that do not conform to its peculiar logic. Similarly, I would say that the hegemonic blocs currently in place in the peripheral countries – whose diversity must, of course, be carefully analysed – are of a 'comprador' nature: that is, the interests they promote are situated within the logic of the expansion of global capitalism as it exists today. Here too, however, alternative blocs are possible, and if successful they might compel the global system to adapt to their demands.

In order to make this book read more smoothly, I have decided to group all references to useful complementary sources in an appendix.

CHAPTER 1

The triad: America, Europe and Japan
– united or fragmented?

The phase of the global deployment of capitalism, which began in 1945 but was impeded until the collapse of the post-war social orders (welfare state, Sovietism, national populism in the South), is characterized by the emergence of a collective imperialism. The 'triad' (that is, the United States plus its Canadian external province, Europe west of the Polish frontier, and Japan – to which we should add Australia and New Zealand) defines the area of this collective imperialism. It 'manages' the economic dimension of capitalist globalization through the institutions at its service (WTO, IMF, World Bank, OECD), and the political–military dimension through Nato, whose responsibilities have been redefined so that it can in effect substitute itself for the United Nations.

Yet the current moment in this phase is also characterized by a US offensive to impose its own leadership on the triad, involving a conception of 'military control of the planet' worked out by the George W. Bush administration. The question that immediately arises is whether this is a viable conception. Are the triad partners forced to accept US leadership, either in the stark forms unilaterally decided by Washington or with some 'concessions' that allow for a less unbalanced division of responsibilities and benefits? Or are we heading towards a radical, if gradual, challenge to Atlanticism (and the complementary asymmetrical alliance between the USA and Japan), and therefore towards the breaking up of the triad? In both cases, we need to be clear what the different developments would entail for North–South relations.

In the immediate term, the United States enjoys an evident strategic advantage: its project is the only one that is clearly and openly formulated and, by virtue of the initiatives taken by Washington, the only one that is actually in play. Up to now its partners in the international community – the triad allies and the rest – have done nothing more than respond to those initiatives, whether by falling into line, accepting with bad grace or seeking to limit some of the consequences they find most troubling to themselves. None has a really positive alternative to guide its strategy, and in a thoroughly disorganized manner each places the immediate emphasis on what it considers to be the defence of its own interests.

The question we posed does not admit of a simple answer, for the contemporary world has been undergoing a number of massive changes. Europe, now the largest trading power, has embarked on a common project of political construction that will probably rule out a return to the internecine wars of its past. Japan has become a major economic power, and a large part of Asia is heading along the road of accelerated development. The United States, for its part, has made a sensational comeback, while the disappearance of 'actually existing socialism' has helped to spread the idea that capitalism is the only possible future for all nations. In these conditions, the geometry of possible rapprochement among the different poles of power and wealth has become extremely complex.

To see our way more clearly, we may usefully start by analysing the project of the US ruling class and identifying its strengths and weaknesses. Then we shall consider how Europe – or the different Europes – and Japan are responding to the challenge, and which conditions need to be fulfilled if the various options of the triad partners are to take effect. This analysis will allow us to clarify the nature of possible conflicts within the triad, and to identify the terrain on which they might occur. It will also enable us to begin discussion on what the various scenarios would entail for North–South relations.

The project of the American ruling class: extension of the Monroe doctrine to the rest of the world

The project that the US ruling class has cherished since 1945 now has five objectives: (i) to neutralize and subjugate the other triad partners (Europe and Japan) and to minimize their capacity to act outside the

American fold; (ii) to establish military control over Nato and to 'Latin Americanize' the former parts of the Soviet world; (iii) to assert undivided control over the Middle East and its oil resources; (iv) to break up China, to ensure the subordination of the other major states (India, Brazil), and to prevent the constitution of any regional blocs that might renegotiate the terms of globalization; and (v) to marginalize regions in the South that are of no strategic interest.

The project, which was devised after Potsdam and grounded on the American nuclear monopoly, has always assigned a key role to its military dimension. In a very short time the United States put in place a global military strategy, divided the globe into a number of regions, and created several 'Military Commands' to take responsibility for each. The aim was not only to encircle the USSR (and China) but also to make Washington the worldwide master of last resort: in other words, to extend to the whole planet the Monroe doctrine that had already staked its claim to run the New World in accordance with its own 'national interests'.

The main instrument in the current US drive for hegemony is therefore military. Such hegemony would in turn guarantee that of the triad over the global system, but the allies of the United States would have to accept their subaltern status, as Britain and Japan already do, and to recognize its necessity without feeling even any 'cultural' qualms. This means, however, that the talk of economic strength with which European politicians regale their local constituencies would lose all purchase on reality. If Europe places itself entirely on the ground of mercantile disputes, without advancing any project of its own, it will have been defeated in advance. People in Washington are well aware of that.

The project implies that the 'sovereign national interests of the United States' should hold sway over all other principles defining what is regarded as legitimate political behaviour; it leads to systematic distrust of all international law.

The ruling class of the United States freely proclaims that it will not 'tolerate' the reconstitution of any economic or military power capable of challenging its global domination. To this end, it has given itself the right to wage 'preventive wars', with three main potential adversaries in mind.

First, the dismemberment of the Russian Federation, following that of the USSR, is a major strategic objective for the United States. Until now the Russian ruling class does not appear to have understood this. It seemed convinced that, having lost the war, it could go on to win the peace – as Germany and Japan did before it. What it forgot was that Washington needed the recovery of its two wartime enemies, precisely in order to face down the Soviet challenge. The new conjuncture is different, as the United States no longer has a serious rival. Its option is therefore to destroy its defeated Russian adversary once and for all. Has Putin finally understood this? Is Russia beginning to shake off its illusions?

Second, the huge size and economic success of China are such that the United States is seriously worried, and here too has a strategic goal of dismembering the country.

Europe comes third in the list, as seen by the new lords of the earth. Up to now, however, the North American establishment does not appear to be so uneasy about its relations with Europe. The unconditional Atlanticism of some countries (Britain and the EU's new servile members in the East), the 'shifting sands' of Europeanism itself, the convergent interests of dominant capital within the triad's collective imperialism: all this is tending to roll back the European project, or to maintain it as the European 'section' of the US project. Washington's diplomatic efforts have managed to keep Germany in tow; the reunification and conquest of Eastern Europe have even appeared to strengthen the Atlantic alliance, as Germany has ostensibly been encouraged to resume its traditional *Drang nach Osten* (witness Berlin's role in breaking up Yugoslavia through the hasty recognition of Slovenian and Croatian independence) and otherwise asked to steer in the American wake. Is a change of course currently under way? The German political class appears hesitant, perhaps divided, in its choice of strategy.

The alternative to Atlanticist alignment calls instead for the strengthening of a Paris–Berlin–Moscow axis, which could become the backbone of a European system independent of Washington.

The prevailing opinion is that US military power is only the tip of the iceberg, prolonging its economic as well as political and cultural superiority. In my view, however, the United States has no decisive economic advantages within the system of collective imperialism; on the contrary, scarcely any of its sectors could be certain of seeing off competitors in the kind of truly open market imagined by liberal economists. Evidence of this is the fact that the US trade deficit keeps growing year after year, having soared from $100 billion in 1989 to $500 billion in 2002, and that this deficit involves practically every segment of the productive system. The competition between Ariane and Nasa space rockets, or between Airbus and Boeing, testifies to the vulnerability of the American advantage. Indeed, without extra-economic means that violate the 'liberal' principles imposed on its rivals, the United States would probably not be able to compete with Europe or Japan in high technology, with China, Korea and other industrial countries of Asia and Latin America in ordinary manufactured products, or with Europe and the Southern Cone of Latin America in agriculture.

The US economy lives as a parasite off its partners in the global system, with virtually no national savings of its own. The world produces while North America consumes. The advantage of the United States is that of a predator whose deficit is covered by what others agree, or are forced, to contribute. Washington uses various means to make up for its deficiencies: for example, repeated violations of the principles of liberalism, arms exports, and the hunting down of oil super-profits (which involves the periodic felling of producers: one of the real motives behind the wars in Central Asia and Iraq). But the fact is that the bulk of the American deficit is covered by capital inputs from Europe and Japan, China and the South, rich oil-producing countries and comprador classes from all regions, including the poorest, in the Third World – to which should be added the debt-service levy that is imposed on nearly every country in the periphery of the global system. The American superpower depends from day to day on the flow of capital that sustains the parasitism of its economy and society. The vulnerability of the United States therefore represents a serious danger for Washington's project.

The hegemonist strategy of the United States, which operates within the framework of the new collective imperialism, seeks nothing less than to establish Washington's military control over the entire planet. This is the means to ensure privileged access to all of the world's natural resources, and to compel subaltern allies, Russia, China and the whole third world to swallow their status as vassals. Military control of the planet is the means to impose, as a last resort, the draining of 'tribute' through political violence – as a substitute for the 'spontaneous' flow of capital that offsets the American deficit, the Achilles heel of US hegemony. The aim of this strategy is neither to ensure open markets for all (which exist only in the propaganda of neoliberal sycophants) nor, of course, to make democracy prevail throughout the world.

Europe in particular, but also the rest of the world, will have to choose between two strategies: either to invest their 'surplus capital' ('savings') in financing the US consumption, investment and military expenditure deficit; or to use the surplus as a boost for the economy in their own countries. As it is, the transfusion requires Europeans to bow to 'deflationary' policies (a term improperly used in mainstream economics: I would prefer to say 'stagnationary'), the function of which is to release a surplus of exportable savings. It makes a (still weak) recovery in Europe depend on the artificially sustained recovery of the United States. Conversely, the mobilization of this surplus for local jobs in Europe would provide a simultaneous boost to consumption (by reviving the social dimension of economic management devastated by the neoliberal virus) and investment (especially in new technology and R&D, or even military expenditure, by putting an end to the US 'advantage' in this field). This kind of response to the challenge would establish a new equilibrium of social relations in favour of the working classes; conflicts between countries would thus be combined with social struggles. In other words, the US–Europe opposition is not fundamentally about a clash of interests between the dominant segments of capital in the different partners.

The neoliberal option for Europe, reinforced by a supposedly 'non-political' management of its common currency (the euro), is a major handicap for any strategy to lift the continent clear of stagnation. This absurd monetary policy suits Washington down to the ground, since the US currency (the dollar) is managed in a quite different, thoroughly political manner that has nothing to do with neoliberal dogma. Combined with the possibility that Washington will gain exclusive control over the world's oil reserves, it ensures that what I call the oil/dollar standard will remain in the end the sole international monetary instrument, relegating the euro to the status of a subaltern regional currency.

The political conflict that might oppose Europe (or some major European countries) to the United States does not stem from fundamental disagreements expressing a clash of interests between dominant capitals. I would locate it, rather, within the conflict between different 'national interests' and profoundly different political cultures. My answer to whether the triad is united or fragmented may therefore be summarized in a single sentence. The dominant economic tendency operates in favour of triad unity, whereas politics points towards the break-up of triad unity, because of the diversity of national interests and political cultures.

The shifting sands of the European project

Up to now, all the governments of European countries have rallied to the theses of economic liberalism. This has meant nothing less than the eclipse of the European project, a dilution both economic (the advantages of the EU dissolved into globalization) and political (disappearing political and military autonomy). As things stand today, there is no European project. It has been replaced with a North Atlantic (or triad) project under American command.

Wars 'made in the USA' have certainly woken public opinion (especially in Europe against the latest war, in Iraq) and even some governments (especially the French, but also the German, Russian and Chinese). Yet these same governments have not reconsidered their loyal attachment to the requirements of 'liberalism'. This adds up to a major contradiction, which will have to be overcome in one way or the other: either by bowing to Washington's demands or by making a real break that puts an end to Atlanticism.

My main political conclusion from this analysis is that Europe cannot break out of Atlanticism so long as the political alliances that define its ruling blocs remain centred on dominant transnational capital. Only if social and political struggles succeed in changing the make-up of those blocs and imposing new compromises between capital and labour will Europe be able to take some distance from Washington and make possible a renewal of the European project. This being so, Europe could – and should – also strike out independently in the sphere of relations with the East and South, taking a different path that goes beyond the mere requirements of collective imperialism and begins the long march 'beyond capitalism'. In other words, either Europe will be a left Europe (in a serious sense of 'left') or we can forget about any 'European project'.

The European project was conceived after the Second World War as part of the US Atlantic project, in the spirit of the 'cold war', and the European bourgeoisies, weakened and fearful of their own working classes, signed up to it more or less unconditionally.

Despite the dubious origins, however, the actual deployment of the project has gradually modified a number of important factors and challenges. The countries of Western Europe have succeeded in 'catching up' the United States both economically and technologically, or have the means to do so. The Soviet 'enemy' is no longer there. And the violent hostilities that marked European history for a century and a half have given way to reconciliation among the three main continental countries, France, Germany and Russia. All these trends are positive, and contain an even more positive potential. It is true that economic liberalism has inspired the basis of the project, but until the 1980s this was tempered by a 'social-democratic historic compromise' that forced capital to adapt to the demand for social justice expressed by the working classes. Since then, the project has developed in a new social framework inspired by American-style anti-social liberalism.

This shift has plunged European societies into a multidimensional crisis. First, there is simply the economic crisis built into the liberal option, a crisis deepened by Europe's alignment with the North American leader and its agreement to fund the US deficit at the expense of its own interests. Then there is the social crisis, which has grown sharper through the rise of popular resistance and class struggles against the baneful consequences of the neoliberal turn. Finally, there are the beginnings of a political crisis, visible in the refusal to fall unconditionally into line with the US perspective of endless war against the South.

How are the peoples and governments of Europe facing up to this threefold challenge? Those who are Europeanist by principle divide into three rather different groups:

- Those who support the neoliberal orientation and more or less unconditionally accept US leadership.
- Those who support the neoliberal orientation but would like to see a politically independent Europe break from its alignment with America.
- Those who would like to see (and who fight for) a 'social Europe' – that is, a capitalism tempered by a new Europe-wide social compromise between capital and labour – and a political Europe that practises

different (friendly, democratic and peaceful) relations with the South, Russia and China. Public opinion throughout Europe has expressed its sympathy for such a position on a number of occasions, at the European Social Forum (Florence 2002, Paris 2003 and London 2004) and in opposition to the war in Iraq.

On what forces are these three currents based? What are their respective chances of success?

The dominant forces of capital are economically liberal by nature and therefore logically support the first option. Tony Blair represents the most consistent expression of what I have called the 'collective triad imperialism'. Politicians who line up behind the star-spangled banner are prepared, if necessary, to sacrifice the European project, or at least to dispel any illusions in connection with it, by keeping it within its original straitjacket as the European part of the Atlanticist project.

For this reason the second option – the one pursued by the two powerful European governments of France and Germany – is difficult to sustain. Does it express the aims of a capital sufficiently strong to break loose from US tutelage? I have no answer to this question. It may possibly be the case, but intuitively I would say that this is not very likely.

And yet those who support this option are allies against the North American adversary, the main enemy of humanity as a whole. I call them allies because I am convinced that, if they persist in this option, they will be led to break from submission to the unilateral project of capital (neoliberalism) and to look leftward for the only forces that can give strength to their project of independence from Washington. An alliance between this second group and the third is not an impossibility, any more than was the broad alliance against Nazism.

Given that Europeanists are incapable of seeing anything else as their priority area of activity, could and should such an alliance operate only within a European framework? I do not believe so. For that framework, such as it is and will continue to be, is systematically favourable only to the orientation of the first, pro-American group. So, will it be necessary to break Europe up and to abandon the pan-European project? I do not think that is either necessary or desirable. Another possible strategy is to put the European project on hold for a while, at its present stage, and to develop other alliances in parallel with it.

Here I would make the first priority the construction of a Paris–Berlin–Moscow political and strategic alliance, extended if possible to Beijing and Delhi. It would be political because its aim would be to revive international pluralism and all the functions of the UN; and it would be strategic because it would seek to rebuild military strength at a level required by the challenge of the United States. These three or four powers have the technological and financial means to go through with it, and even the United States pales beside their traditional capacities in the military arena. The American challenge, and Washington's criminal designs, make such a course necessary. Those designs have been stretched to the point of immoderation – but that has to be proved. The creation of a front against hegemonism is the number one priority today, as the creation of an anti-Nazi alliance was the number one priority yesterday.

No European project can make any progress unless the strategy of the United States is put to flight.

The clash of political cultures

With regard to the differences between 'Europeans' and 'North Americans', I should point out that since 1990 my analyses of the 'empire of chaos' have situated the main conflict between them at the level not of economic interests but of political cultures. When mention is made of 'economic interests', it would be useful to draw a clear distinction between the interests of the dominant segments of capital (the large transnational corporations and their financial vanguard rooted in neo-liberal globalization) and what is meant by the vague term 'national (economic) interests'. If there is a collective imperialism, this is because the dominant segments of capital share common interests in running the globalized system. To be sure, each TNC competes with other TNCs, and each state (none more than the United States) actively supports its own TNCs in the competitive struggle. But the conflicts and alliances in question, which often take shape between transnational blocs of interests, involve variable geometries that should not be reduced to a narrowing or widening of the gap between states.

In my own conception, the state cannot be equated with an agency waiting at the pleasure of the dominant segments of capital. In some conjunctures that may be what it is – or almost. At the present time, for example, political imbalances due to the collapse of post-war historic compromises between capital and labour have turned it into such an agency. But this change is not set to last: it is threatened by the emergent political strength of social interests other than those defended by the dominant capital, and by the consequent reassertion of what we may call 'national interests'. These interests are by no means necessarily a coherent set, although mainstream geopolitical theorists often tend towards such a simplistic view. Involved here are the interests of capital in general (since we are speaking of capitalist societies), which express themselves through the strategies and demands of the 'national' productive system as a whole; defence of these interests mobilizes major sections of the middle classes and therefore has considerable weight in the electoral scales. But there are also the interests of the popular classes, of the working people, which sometimes express themselves forcefully in opposition to those of capital and its claim to speak on behalf of the nation – for example, when a large or not so large section of workers seeks to promote a 'socialist' alternative, or even when they give up that goal and aim merely to win the 'share of the cake' to which they feel entitled. This latter distinction already allows us to draw a dividing line between the United States and Europe. For, whereas the American trade unionism inspired by Samuel Gompers does not challenge capitalism even in a long-term perspective, other traditions are the rule in Europe, however much they may also differ from country to country or period to period.

This brings us to the question of political cultures. The term 'political' here marks out my own theoretical position: I do not speak of 'cultures' in general, in the manner of the fashionable discourse of 'difference'; what I mean by political culture is a complex outcome of historical social struggles in the country in question, combined with the international conflicts that define the place of the nation in the global order.

Within this conceptual framework, I have defined the political culture or cultures of Europe (or of a large part of the continent) as the historical outcome of four elements: (i) the philosophy of the Enlightenment; (ii) the 'bourgeois revolutions' that ushered in modernity, especially the most radical of them, the French Revolution, which was at once a bourgeois revolution and a people's revolution; (iii) the early rise of the workers' movement (in all its 'reformist' and 'revolutionary' tendencies) that made its mark on the nineteenth and twentieth centuries; and (iv) the impact of the Russian Revolution and the resulting break between Communists and Social Democrats. The complex outcome of this itinerary shaped the left/right divide peculiar to Europe, as it shaped basic concepts of society that combined the conflicting values of liberty and equality and the practices of a secular democracy where the notion of citizenship occupied a central place.

The political culture of the United States was formed in quite a different way. To begin with, of course, there was the foundation of New England by the religious émigrés – which means that analysis of the various dimensions of the Reformation has an importance in America that it does not have in relation to later European history. The Reformation, we may say, was the expression of various reactions by social classes to the challenge of nascent capitalism, and one of those reactions was that of layers who suffered from changes associated with the rise of new social relations. These victims – 'the poor' – generated a religious ideology that rejected the Enlightenment. The American ideology was thus, in its initial nucleus, not a variant of the Enlightenment but a protest against it. It is this which allows us to understand why the social and cultural life of the United States has passed through an unfailing succession of 'Salem witch episodes'. Every fifty years or so the country experiences a 'moral crisis' of this type, and takes refuge in a make-believe 'defence of Good against Evil' that is absent from the history of Europe. McCarthyism in the 1950s and the neo-conservative revolution under way today are two expressions of this ideological persistence.

The second element peculiar to the formation of American political culture stems from the role of waves of immigration in constituting its working classes (urbanized workers as well as those who conquered the West). In each successive generation, the crystallization of a European-style labour movement was thereby prevented. What crystallized instead was multiple forms of 'communitarianism'.

The other formative elements of American political culture – slavery and its racist legacy, the Indian genocide and the contempt for other peoples that it expressed – are equally specific and have no parallel in Europe. Whether based on slavery or not, Europe's colonies (though often associated with massacres) remained outside its own continent.

Finally, the political culture of the United States produced a system of concepts very different from those found in Europe. Its concept of liberty places a distinctive emphasis on free enterprise, while also attaching a comparatively low value to equality. Unlike Europe – which has gone further in this sense – it has never understood the secular principle as anything more than tolerance of religious diversity.

This political culture serves wonderfully to ensure the undivided and internalized rule of capital, which in Europe often has to remain constantly on its guard. The US system is well-nigh perfect for this purpose: its presidency and 'single party' (split between Democrats and Republicans) succeed in warding off the potential danger contained elsewhere in the practice of electoral democracy.

As it took shape, the political culture of capitalism defined a number of rights and developed its own distinctive conception of law and democracy; the contours of this stand out clearly from an analysis of the mode of thought still prevalent in the United States, where the culture appears in the form least contaminated by the culture of its victims and opponents. Originally, the only recognized rights were those of individuals (even the personality of 'corporations' only came later), and in reality the individuals in question were 'white men', to the exclusion of women and slaves (among whom we may also include the colonized peoples). The 'contract' between individuals therefore had primacy over the law, so that the legislative role of the state was relegated to the sidelines; the result is that in the United States a quite ordinary 'contract' may run to two hundred pages or more, while in Europe (where the law has primacy) a couple of pages suffice. These basic elements accompany a political culture rooted in a strict division between the realm of economic life (where private property and freedom for property-owners hold sway, ignoring social dimensions and devaluing equality) and the realm of political life. The latter thus shrinks to the mere practice of 'representative democracy' – that is, to the formula of 'party competition plus elections' – which rules out any more advanced (by definition, participatory) form of democracy. The concept of 'civil society' then crowns it all. For, in its American sense, this comes down to no more than an amorphous bunch of 'apolitical' NGOs which, especially in the majority case of organizations with a 'communitarian' religious, para-religious, ethnic or neighbourhood basis, are supposed to resemble the private business sector, though 'closer to the public' (itself conceived as made up consumers rather than citizens) and hence more effective in the management of public goods such as education and health. The fact that such procedures serve further to deepen inequalities is not seen as a problem, especially since the aspiration to equality does not figure as an important ethical value.

Since the French Revolution, the political cultures of France and continental Europe, though existing within a perfectly capitalist framework, have been considerably different from the one we have just described. Here, the values of liberty and equality have from the beginning been placed on an equal footing, and this has required social management of the conflict between the two, and state action to regulate the deployment of capitalism in that light. This different approach opens up the possibility – if social struggles make it necessary – of making a start on participatory democracy. By their very nature, such moves accentuate the conflict with the inherent tendencies of capital accumulation, since a majority of citizens may then oppose the minority of 'property-owners' who alone count as real active citizens under the exclusive logic of capitalism. The way is thus opened to a recognition of positive social rights, which the American liberal model ignores in principle on the grounds that they require active intervention by the legislative and executive, as opposed to mere political and civil liberties that require the state only to refrain from impeding their use. In the European model, then, the idea of public services (health, education) requiring collective management to ensure maximum equality has come to occupy a major place in the running of society. That this approach is more efficient than the one associated with liberalism is shown by a comparison of health spending (a much smaller proportion of GDP in Europe, compared to the USA) and by the far better results achieved in Europe. Against this background, a different concept of civil society has become possible, one that recognizes the importance of labour unions and other popular movements to defend social rights and various kinds of politicized civil organization. This political culture points beyond the limits inherent in the logic of capitalist expansion, in such a way that the socialist future already exists as a potentiality within the capitalist present.

The conflict between the culture of the past and the culture of the future has been opened by Washington's offensive to impose its shrivelled and regressive vision on the whole planet. Its ambitions are all the more

arrogant since the English common law underlying its juridical infrastructure is a primitive form that has been largely superseded elsewhere,
both in Europe and in many countries of the South. Yet the goal has been
clearly declared: United States law must be accepted as a substitute for
international law. Moscow's aim of foisting on others a socialism reduced
to the Soviet model is by now a thing of the past, but a glance at the
language of contemporary politics and the media is enough to highlight
the retreat that has already been registered in the battle now upon us. The
vanished terms: state, politics, power, classes, class struggle, social change,
alternatives and revolutions, ideologies. Their insipid replacements: governance, communities, social partners, poverty, consensus, alternation.

Will the contrast between the political cultures of the United States
and Europe withstand Americanization of the old continent? In this
connection, the draft constitution for the European Union was highly
disturbing: it set in stone both economic liberalism and the Nato functions underpinning Atlanticism, and its Article 51 enshrined the role of
the churches in the life of society. Sounding the death knell of secularism,
it called for adaptation to American-style conceptions of the place of
religion in society, for the acceptance of sects and fundamentalist movements as an ordinary part of the landscape, and for the crystallization
of communalist tendencies. This obscurantist breakthrough was a great
success for Opus Dei: its reactionary ideology inspired the authors of the
draft and, most especially, Giscard d'Estaing, whose aim is to erase the
Enlightenment, the French Revolution and socialism from the European
memory. Had it been accepted, the only remaining reason for conflict
among the triad partners would be divergences of national interests, with
no basis in a diversity of political cultures.

In my view, this is the ground on which the 'clash of civilizations' between the United States and Europe is situated. In Europe (and large parts
of the rest of the world) it is the same as the conflict between capitalism
and socialism – a conflict that does not exist in the United States.

And Japan?

Readers will remember the waves of enthusiasm which, twenty or so years
ago, cast Japan as the rising hegemon that would eventually supplant the
United States. Japan the inventor of new forms of labour ('Toyotism'),

Japan in the forefront of research and development, Japan the great saver buying up American industry! Such ideas never made much impression on me, as they seemed to disregard the structural weaknesses of the Empire of the Rising Sun.

First there is Japan's geographical position, which makes it a prisoner of the United States. This was true in relation to the USSR, a major military power and potential enemy that has now disappeared. And it is true in relation to China, which – like Korea even – will never agree for a moment to follow in Tokyo's wake.

Next, the success of Japan's industrial development and export drive, so impressive at the time in comparison with Europe and the United States, did not in any way guarantee that it would move into a hegemonic position. Investment of Japan's external trade surplus in the United States always struck me as a sign of weakness rather than strength, for it was the result of economic policies imposed by Washington, in order to force a subaltern ally to finance, and offset, the inadequacies of its 'rival' and master. In just the same way, the EU's surplus today is the result of de-flationary policies within the EU that serve to enhance North American interests, allowing Washington to pursue an expansionist policy without sufficient means of its own to fund it. Japanese and European surpluses, American deficits: these are two sides of a coin that spells leadership for the United States and dependent adjustment for its partners.

Lastly, Japan's political culture did not prepare its people for the tasks that fall to a global hegemon. The reason for this is not its unfamiliarity with the requirements of democracy, beyond formal elections in favour of the ruling conservative party – after all, that way of politically running the country largely resulted from subservience to the American master. The point, rather, is that the political culture that has taken shape since the Meiji Restoration does not prepare the popular classes to challenge the social order on which the stability of the system depends. In contrast to modern China, which is the product of a radical revolution, Japan exerts no attraction worth mentioning over the peoples of Asia.

The Japanese model, adapted to global conjunctural trends over which it had no control, was always likely to enter a deep crisis once the con-juncture turned for the worse. Moreover, the stagnation that has affected the Japanese economy for more than ten years produces virtually no response, either from the ruling class or from the people, that offers any light at the end of the tunnel. Responsibility for the future is entrusted entirely to 'the world', and principally to the American leader.

In the foreseeable future, then, it is hard to imagine that Japan will play an active role in reconstructing the global system. Most probably, it will be carried along by Washington's militarist project – unless the popular classes enter the arena and, through the intensification of their struggles, begin to develop a challenge to the system. Meanwhile Japanese capital can derive only modest profits from the alignment with the United States, and these might be further limited by concessions that Washington imposes on Tokyo with regard to the exploitation of Southeast Asia's natural resources and cheap labour.

CHAPTER 2

Does the rise of China challenge
the imperialist order?

China's rise: revolution or opening to the world?

The prevailing opinion today is that Asia is overcoming the legacy of underdevelopment due to imperialism and 'closing the gap' within the capitalist system, through methods that do not involve a break with that system. Appearances seem to confirm this vision of the future, since over the last quarter of a century Asia has notched up truly remarkable growth rates at a time when the rest of the world has been sliding deeper into stagnation. A linear projection might therefore suggest that we are heading for a renewal of the globalized capitalist system, which will be more balanced in favour of Asia, a capitalism that thereby loses its imperialist character at least in relation to East and South Asia, if not the rest of the third world. We might add for good measure that the region disposes of sizeable military capacities (currently undergoing modernization), and that China and India are both nuclear powers.

It is supposed to be certain that this is leading to a multipolar world, organized around four poles of at least potentially equivalent military and economic strength (USA, EU, Japan, China), or perhaps as many as six (including Russia and India). All these poles together, plus the countries and regions directly associated with them (Canada, non-EU Europe, Southeast Asia, Korea), encompass the great majority of peoples on earth. The argument is, therefore, that such a multipolar system would differ both from the successive deployments of multipolar imperialism (up to

1945) and from the subsequent unipolar (collective triad) imperialism, which encompassed only a minority of the world's peoples.

The reasoning behind this vision seems inadequate in a number of ways. First of all, it does not take account of the policies that Washington intends to deploy against the Chinese project; nor does it see that, since Europe is still unable to imagine a break with the Atlanticism that keeps it in America's wake, and since Japan, for similar or special reasons, remains deferential to its protector across the Pacific, the days of collective triad imperialism are still far from numbered. Second, it is deceptive to measure success purely in terms of economic growth rates, especially as it is doubtful whether they can be projected more than a few years into the future. A continuation of Asia's growth will depend on numerous internal and external factors, variously connected with the strategic models of social modernization pursued by local ruling classes and with the reactions of the outside world (that is, of the imperialist powers making up the triad). If there is to be sustained, long-term growth capable of significantly improving Asian living standards, and therefore of guaranteeing the national solidarity that is such a positive legacy of the revolutions in China and Vietnam, then the necessary economic options and political instruments will have be developed in accordance with a coherent plan; they will not arise spontaneously within the current models influenced by capitalist, neoliberal dogma. We may add that a considerable rise in energy consumption (especially of oil) would also be needed; and one result of this – apart from the impact on the global ecological balance – would be an inevitable sharpening of the conflict with the imperialist triad, which up to now has been the sole beneficiary of the resources of the planet.

The prevailing wisdom attributes the success of post-Maoist China entirely to the virtues of the market and the opening to the outside world. Such talk, however, grossly simplifies the reality of Maoist China and sweeps under the carpet the problems posed by the capitalist option. During the three decades of Maoism (1950 to 1980), China already notched up growth rates double those of India or any large region of the third world; the performance of the last two decades of the twentieth century appears all the more extraordinary in that light. No major region in the world has ever done better before. It must be stressed, however, that these unparalleled achievements would not have been possible without the economic, political and social foundations that had been built up in the preceding period, and that the growth acceleration went together with a leap forward in consumption. In other words, whereas the priority in the Maoist period was to build up a solid long-term foundation for the economy, the new economic policy has concentrated on an immediate improvement in consumption made possible by that earlier effort. It is not absurd to argue that the Maoist decades involved a distortion for the sake of building up long-term foundations. But, conversely, the emphasis placed on light industry and services since 1980 cannot last indefinitely, as China is still at a stage that requires expansion of its basic industries.

The issue of openness – that is, participation in the international division of labour and all other aspects of economic globalization (recourse to foreign capital, technology imports, membership in the institutions that run the global economy) and even ideological and cultural globalization – cannot be resolved through the kind of extreme polemical opposition between openness and closure to which dogmatic supporters of neoliberalism usually try to reduce the debate.

To benefit from openness, one must know how to manage it. To speed up development so that it involves a degree of catching up, it is necessary to borrow the most advanced technologies and, in some cases, even to import whole plant – and these have to be paid for out of exports. What can actually be offered on the world market, at this stage of development, is obviously goods that enjoy a 'comparative advantage' by virtue of their high labour intensity. But those who opt for such exports have to understand that they are being exploited by the unequal exchange, even if they accept it for the time being because they lack any alternative. The danger appears when the success of this option leads to a reversal of the sequence that logically governs any development strategy worthy of the name: that is, a strategy involving subordination of quantitative foreign-trade targets to development goals that underpin social solidarity inside the country and, on that basis, strengthen its capacity to make itself felt outside with the maximum degree of autonomy. Liberal dogma proposes the exact opposite: that is, maximum insertion in the international division of labour, based mainly on expansion of those activities for which the country enjoys the comparative advantage of cheap labour. The first option is what I describe as 'delinking', which means not autarky but refusal to bow to the dominant logic of the world capitalist system; the second option is one of inevitably passive adaptation (even if it is called 'active insertion') to the demands of integration into the global system.

If China remains stuck with the option chosen by those in power today, its growth rates will tail off until they reach the level of India's. The central question is therefore whether China is evolving towards a stable form of capitalism, or whether the perspective still exists of a transition to socialism. What we need to know is whether the ruling class can reach the goals it has set for itself, what are likely to be the special, or not so special, characteristics of the Chinese capitalism now under construction, and, in particular, what degree of stability it is likely to achieve. What are the possibilities for the capitalist road in China today? Alliances are already in place that draw together the state authorities, the new class of 'big private capitalists', the peasantry in areas grown rich through the proximity of urban markets, and the rapidly advancing middle classes. But the fact remains that this hegemonic bloc excludes the great majority of workers and peasants. It would therefore be shaky and artificial to draw any analogy with the alliances that certain European bourgeoisies forged with the peasantry (against the working class), or with social democracy's later historic compromise between labour and capital.

In the context of triad imperialism, forms of the centre–core opposition based on the new monopolies are bound to deepen, rather than alleviate, the polarization on a world scale. This being so, the term 'emergent economies' is the stuff of ideological farce: it is a question of countries which, far from 'catching up', are engaged in building the peripheral capitalism of tomorrow. China is no exception in this respect.

In contrast to this model, which corresponds to a new stage in the deployment of capitalism within a still imperialist framework, the long road towards the socialist alternative will be different from the ones imagined by the Second and Third Internationals. 'Market socialism' might be an initial phase along that road, but it would have to fulfil certain conditions for that to be so. Here, the agrarian question is at the heart of the challenge facing contemporary China.

Market socialism: transition, or short-cut to capitalism?

1. The basic question to be asked is the same as in 1980, when China, under Deng Xiaoping, began its turn to that form of 'market economy'

which has led it to where it is today. Ten years before the disappearance of the USSR, I was already asking this question on the basis of a critique of the Soviet model of so-called 'actually existing socialism'. The question is still open today, and it will certainly remain so for a long time to come. But it has to be – or should be – a central preoccupation for anyone who does not identify capitalism with some human rationality present throughout or 'at the end of' history, and who therefore remains eager to think beyond the system, to the exigencies and possibilities involved in the building of a new, and superior, socialist society.

History is often longer than we think, or than we would wish. The first wave of ostensibly socialist experiments, which occupied the major part of the twentieth century, gradually exhausted their potential and either collapsed or began to call themselves into question. A second wave will certainly appear, and it may not be a remake of the one that went before: not only because some lessons must be learned from the defeats but also because in the meantime the capitalist world has changed. After all, the first wave of capitalist transformations, in the Italian cities of the Renaissance, well and truly ended in failure, but the second wave, located in the north-west Atlantic quarter of Europe, resulted in the historical capitalism whose essential forms have remained the same down to the present day.

The debate on the future of socialism is therefore still lively and central. Of course, it can and should be taken up from the several different angles that an always complex and diverse social reality itself offers for analysis and transformative action. Here I shall address it only through some reflections on the possible evolution of China. But the same question is posed elsewhere, on the basis of the experiences of Vietnam and Cuba or the ex-Soviet world, or those of social democracy in the developed capitalist countries, or those of radical national populism in the third world.

My central question is the following. Is China evolving towards a stable form of capitalism? Or is there still a possible perspective of a transition to socialism? I approach the question not in terms of 'forecasting' the most likely eventuality, but in an altogether different way. Which contradictions and struggles have taken centre stage in contemporary China? What are the strengths and weaknesses of the largely capitalist road that has been adopted? What are the strong cards in the hand of anti-capitalist, at least potentially socialist, forces? Under what conditions can the capitalist road emerge victorious, and what form of more or less stable capitalism might it engender? Under what conditions might the present period turn into a long stage in the still longer transition to socialism?

A militant approach, which seeks to place its analytic capacities at the service of transformative action, cannot avoid making predictions, if only because it has to weigh up the consequences of the line that it criticizes or defends. But it cannot remain content to 'predict the future', in the way in which a detached observer thinks he is able to do. The main preoccupation is always to know how the course of history can be affected, and for that it is necessary to go well beyond a mere reading of evolutionary trends.

2. The Chinese ruling class has chosen the capitalist road, if not already with Deng, then at least since his disappearance from the scene. But it does not admit that this is what it has done, because it draws all its legitimacy from a revolution that it cannot repudiate without committing suicide. The Chinese Revolution, like the French Revolution, was the major event, the decisive break, in the history of the nation. It is to these revolutions, imperfect and in some respects even disappointing as they were, that the Chinese and French peoples owe their massive and conscious entry into the arena of their own history. They are 'sacred' revolutions, even if, in both cases, a number of reactionary intellectuals apply themselves to denigrating them, or to denying their real scope.

Yet human beings – and the political forces they represent – should be judged by what they do, not by what they say. The question that must be asked, then, concerns the future of the actual fundamental option in China. The real project of the Chinese ruling class is capitalist in nature, so that 'market socialism' becomes a shortcut enabling it gradually to establish the fundamental structures and institutions of capitalism, by reducing as much as possible the frictions and difficulties of the transition to capitalism. It is at the other end of the spectrum from the method adopted by the Russian ruling class, which agreed to disown the revolution and thereby opened the way for it to become a new bourgeoisie; the Russian method was bound up with the whole logic of 'shock therapy'. It is not clear whether history will allow the Russian ruling class to pull through in this way, and to establish a stable form of capitalism that shores up its class power, at least for a time. We shall return to this in the next chapter.

The Chinese ruling class has embraced a very different option. In my view, a large part of it does realize (and indeed hope) that the line it is pursuing will lead to capitalism, although it may be that a minority remains tied to the rhetoric of 'socialism Chinese-style'. The ruling class also probably knows that its people is attached to 'the values of socialism' (first and foremost, equality) and the real advances associated with them (primarily, equal access to the land for all peasants). It therefore knows that it will have to move towards capitalism with great caution and at a deliberately slow pace.

The question is whether it can achieve its ends, what capitalism Chinese-style might eventually look like, and how stable it would be likely to be. Simply to say that 'the Chinese people will never allow it' is a far from satisfactory answer, although it is not impossible, broadly speaking, that the people will block a capitalist resolution if that is what it wants and if it takes appropriate action. If we are to take the argument further, however, we need a deeper analysis of the contradictions of the capitalist line and its various strengths and weaknesses: what it may be able to offer in terms of growth, development, better social conditions and higher living standards, and what it is not able to offer. Again, it is not much help simply to condemn the capitalist road because it is based on the exploitation of labour. That is true, but it does not prevent capitalism from existing, or even from appearing legitimate to many of those it exploits. The capitalist road derives its strength – as well as much of its legitimacy and stable foundations – from its capacity to achieve economic growth whose material benefits are widely (if unevenly) distributed.

The structure, nature and form of capitalist construction, its degree of stability, are the result of the 'historic compromises' or social alliances that defined the particular succession of hegemonic blocs. Each of the historic roads to capitalism (English, French, German, American…) has produced in turn the distinctive contemporary forms peculiar to each of the capitalist societies in question. It is because these different courses were successfully steered that capitalism is 'stable' (which does not mean eternal!) in the core countries of the world system.

What are the possibilities for the capitalist road in China today? We have already referred to alliances among the state authorities, big

capitalists (still mostly overseas Chinese, but perhaps eventually including a similar class of mainland Chinese), peasants in areas close to
booming urban markets, and the fast-rising middle classes. Indeed, such
alliances are already in existence. But the exclusion of the great majority
of workers and peasants is a weakness of the pro-capitalist hegemonic
bloc in China, and lies at the root of its problems of political management. We can leave it to crude American ideologues to place an equals
sign between market and democracy. The reality is that, under certain
conditions, capitalism functions in parallel with a given democratic form
so long as it can control its uses and prevent the (anti-capitalist) 'devia-
tions' that democracy inevitably involves. But, when it is incapable of
doing this, capitalism simply dispenses with democracy and is none the
worse for it.

In China, the legacy of the Third International (Leninist and Maoist
Marxism) and its conceptions of 'dictatorship of the proletariat' and
so-called 'socialist democracy' means that the democratic question is
posed in more complex forms. I have dealt with this elsewhere and will
not address it again here. But it is evident that political forms derived
from the Third International are not easily compatible with a capitalist
option that appears more and more openly as capitalist. How will the
Party-State be able to keep its name (Communist Party) and its reference,
however purely rhetorical, to Marx and Mao? Under present conditions
in China, could it work to abandon them in favour of the forms of
'Western democracy' (above all, a multiparty electoral system)? It is
doubtful: not for supposedly historical para-cultural reasons ('democracy
is an alien concept in Chinese culture', etc.), but because the social
struggles that threaten to mobilize the popular classes would make the
practice of such forms untenable. China has to invent a different form of
democracy, in association with market socialism understood as a phase in
the long socialist transition. Otherwise, it is hard to see anything other
than the succession of illegitimate autocracies and unstable 'low-grade
democracies' that is the current lot of the capitalist third world.

The economic possibilities for the capitalist road in China, as well
as the range of political management options associated with them, also
depend, at least in part, on the conditions under which such a capitalism is inserted into the world system of today and tomorrow. It is not a
question only of the economic aspects of this insertion; the geopolitical

aspects are no less important. And, as we know, the United States has already proclaimed – in the voices of Bush Sr, Clinton and Bush Jr – that it will not tolerate the rise of a new Chinese power, even a capitalist one.

Rhetoric concerning the diversity of capitalism is flourishing everywhere in the contemporary world, often in tandem with the incantatory evocation of ill-defined specificities that can be exploited with the maximum degree of political opportunism. China is no exception in this respect, and the 'Chinese road' – tacitly capitalist for some, ostensibly socialist for others – is rarely defined with sufficient precision to escape such opportunist instrumentalization.

Variety is a fact of nature, and references to the diversity of capitalist societies a platitude. Yes, 'Rhineland capitalism' (not to speak of French or German capitalism, still rather different from each other despite the reconciliation) is not the same as 'Anglo-Saxon capitalism' (where the differences are also considerable, on the two sides of the Atlantic). But why is this so? For my part, I have proposed shifting the debate from the level of contemporary description to historical analysis of the social struggles accompanying the formation of modernity that generated the political cultures we know today. Without repeating the arguments, it may be useful to summarize them again with reference to the contrasting ideologies of North America and Europe. The former recognizes only two fundamental values: private property and liberty (understood as the liberty to use property free from any constraint). The latter recognizes a value of equality, whose conflict with the value of liberty has to be managed through certain constraints on property (which the French Revolution then replaced with 'fraternity'). The contrast between these two ideologies is actually at the heart of the contradiction between Europe and the United States, which should not be located at the level of a conflict of interests within dominant capital, since a collective triad imperialism (USA, Europe, Japan) has taken over from the imperialism of earlier history.

Equally if not more important is the opposition between the peripheral capitalisms as a whole (themselves diverse in space and time) and the capitalisms of the core. The form of this opposition has changed between one stage and another of the expansion of a world capitalism, which, though always imperialist (in the sense of polarizing), has continually

grown deeper. At this level, the future is no different from the past and
the present, as polarization is intrinsic to capitalism. We have already
looked at the forms of core–periphery opposition based on a combination of new core monopolies (technology, access to natural resources,
communications and information, control of the world finance system,
weapons of mass destruction), which have been replacing the ordinary
industrial monopoly of earlier times. The capitalism being built in the
so-called 'emergent economies', China among them, does not involve
'catching up' in any of these domains.

Invocation of a cultural or supposedly cultural dimension, and of the
variety that this makes necessary for the roads to capitalism (or socialism), becomes ritualistic in its forms of expression and opportunist in the
ends it seeks to justify, as soon as culture is conceived as a transhistorical
invariable; every fundamentalism, from George W. Bush to Osama bin
Laden, here evades the real issue of the interaction and constant transformation of different cultures, by immediately removing it from the
field of reflection. No less crude is the supposed opposition between
'normal capitalism' (a Weberian ideal type) and 'popular capitalism' (a
much-touted type based on widespread ownership of property, where
citizens are at once workers, shareholders and homeowners). Beyond
all its variants and varieties, whether in the past or future, core or
periphery, capitalism always denotes a society (not only an economy) in
which economistic, market-centred alienation is the intrinsic condition
governing its subordination to the exigencies of accumulation.

3. Socialism is defined first of all as the emancipation of humanity, and
hence as the construction of a general mode of social organization freed
from alienating submission to the exigencies of capital accumulation.
Socialism and democracy are therefore inseparable from each other. I
shall not repeat what I have written elsewhere about the systems in the
Soviet world and Maoist China, their original projects and evolution (or
deformation), the role of circumstances and pressure to 'catch up', or the
responsibility of the ideologies of the labour and socialist movement of
the Second and Third Internationals. I shall simply recall my earlier
warnings against the kind of reductionist confusion that made certain
conceptions of central planning (themselves an appropriate response in
the earliest years) synonymous with 'fully developed socialism'.

'Fully developed socialism' – if such a term can be used to describe any social system – would necessarily be more global than capitalism, whose skewed and truncated globalization generates an inherent polarization between core and periphery. In any event, such a socialism cannot be described in advance in terms of precise forms of organization and appropriate institutions; all that can be specified are certain principles to guide the people's creative imagination and the full exercise of powers that come with an ever deeper but never complete democratization. The kind of creative utopia inspired by Marx or the liberation theologians – and we should accept that to be a Marxist means not stopping but starting with Marx – offers much more food for thought than a mediocre, so-called 'realist' sociology. The road to such a socialism will be long – more protracted than, and different from, those envisaged by the Second and Third Internationals. 'Market socialism' might be a first stage in that direction, but there are three conditions for it to serve that function.

The first is that forms of collective ownership must be created, maintained and strengthened during the process of social advance. These forms can and must be multiple, involving ownership by the state, by regional communities, by workers' collectives and by citizens. But, for them to operate with all the responsibility required for market exchange, they must be conceived as forms of genuine ownership, not as expressions of weakly defined powers. Incidentally, I do not accept here the fashionable simplification, first cooked up by von Mises and Hayek, which conflates property with private property – a confusion that stems from, and situates itself on the same terrain as, the confusion between socialism and Soviet-style central planning. For the dominance of collective property does not rule out the granting of some place to private property: not only local small-scale property (craftspeople, small and medium-sized firms, small businesses and services), but perhaps even large-scale enterprise or arrangements with big transnational capital. But what must always be clearly defined is the framework in which such entities are allowed to operate.

The second condition, then, is that the responsibilities of 'property-owners' (states, collectives, private entities) must be regulated – a rather loose formulation, which can be further specified only with reference to the particular requirements during the stage of social transformation and to the longer-term socialist goal. In other words, we should understand by regulation a conflictual combination between the exigencies of capitalist-style accumulation (in spite of the collective character of the property) and the progressive deployment of the values of socialism (first and foremost: equality, involvement of everyone in the process of change, or public service in the noblest sense of the term).

The third condition concerns democracy, which is evidently insepa-rable from the concept of emancipation. Democracy is not a formula given once and for all, which has only to be 'applied', but an always incomplete process, which makes me think the term 'democratization' would be preferable. Ever richer and more complex forms of democracy must be able to combine the precise 'procedures' that need to be ad-dressed (the rule of law, in simple language), as well as meeting the substantive requirement that the practice of democracy should be capable of reinforcing the impact of the values of socialism on decision-making processes at every level and in every domain.

Could the Soviet system have evolved in that direction and introduced the appropriate reforms, breaking in its way the straitjacket of central planning and a self-appointed state-party 'vanguard'? The question now belongs to history, but in any event the reforms that were eventually envisaged did not point in that direction: on the contrary, they were intended to prolong the life of a system that had reached its historical limits.

China, for its part, has now taken up a position outside the 'market socialism' that we have proposed here; it has been advancing along the capitalist road and accepted, in principle, the substitution of private property for mainly collective public property. Many critics of the present system, especially Chinese people, maintain that it is 'already too late' – and they are not without solid factual arguments to back them up. But that is not exactly my view. As long as equal access to the land continues to be recognized in principle and applied in practice, I think it possible to argue – as does William Hinton, for example – that it is not yet too late for social action to shift the direction in which things are heading. The case for this will be presented in the following section.

4. In the year 2000, the population of China stood at 1,200 million – two-thirds of it (or 800 million) rural. A simple projection over the next

twenty years shows that it would be illusory, indeed dangerous, to think that urbanization can significantly reduce the size of the rural population, even if it manages to reduce it as a proportion of the whole.

Growing by around 1.2 per cent a year, China's population will reach 1,520 million by the year 2020. Let us assume that its industries and modern services in urban areas record fine growth rates of 5 per cent a year; modernization and the need to compete would certainly require the growth to be generated not entirely through extensive accumulation (the 'same industries and services as today', only in greater number) but also through intensive accumulation, including large rises in labour productivity to the tune of 2 per cent a year. The supply of urban jobs would then increase by 3 per cent a year, bringing to 720 million the total numbers who could be absorbed into the urban areas. This figure would include the same absolute numbers as today of people either unemployed or – no small sector – reduced to precarious and informal types of employment. But they would represent a much smaller proportion of the total, which itself would be no mean achievement.

A simple deduction then leaves a total of 800 million rural Chinese in the year 2020 – the same number as today, but constituting 53 per cent (instead of the present 67 per cent) of the total population. If they are forced to migrate to the cities, because they have no access to the land, they will be able to do no more there than swell the ranks of the marginalized shanty population, as has long been the case in the capitalist third world.

A longer-term projection of forty years would confirm this conclusion. For even in the most optimistic scenario, where modernization and industrialization continue to make rapid progress without major hitches due to unfavourable political or economic events and conjunctures inside or outside the country, one can hope for no more than a gradual reduction in the percentage of the rural population, spaced out over at least another hundred years.

This problem is far from unique to China. It concerns the whole of the third world, or 75 per cent of the world's population.

Peasant agriculture engages nearly half of humanity – three billion human beings. It is divided into two sectors: one which, though rarely mechanized, has benefited from the green revolution of fertilizers, pesticides and seed selection, with output rising to between 100 and

500 quintals per worker; and another still at the level before the green revolution, with output around a mere 10 quintals per worker. Capitalist agriculture, governed by the profit principle and located almost entirely in North America, Europe, the Southern Cone and Australasia, employs little more than a few tens of millions of farmers, who do not form a 'peasantry'. But, as a result of mechanization (over which they have a virtual monopoly) and the huge farm areas, their output is between 10,000 and 20,000 quintals of grain equivalent per worker per annum.

Another 20 million modern farms, if they had access both to large cultivable areas (which would be taken from the peasant economy and include the best soil) and to equipment funded by capital markets, could produce the bulk of what solvent urban consumers still purchase from peasant producers. But what would then become of the billions of un-competitive peasant producers? They would be inexorably wiped out, in the space of a few dozen years. What will become of these billions of human beings, most of them already among the world's poor (three-quarters of the world's undernourished are rural dwellers), who presently scrape a living with the utmost difficulty? Over the next fifty years, even if we assume the fantastic hypothesis of 7 per cent annual growth for three-quarters of humanity, no development of industry under more or less competitive conditions could absorb so much as a third of this human reserve. This means that capitalism, by its very nature, is incapable of solving the peasant question, and that the only prospect it offers is of a 'shantyized' planet with billions of surplus human beings.

The strategy that the capitalist rulers now wish to implement involves nothing less than a kind of global 'enclosure'. We have therefore reached the point where, in order to open up new fields for the expansion of capital ('the modernization of agricultural production'), it is necessary to tear whole societies apart. That means 20 million efficient new producers (50 million with their families) on one side; several billion left out in the cold on the other side. The creative side of the operation is a mere drop, compared with the ocean of destruction that it will require. I conclude that capitalism has entered its phase of senile decline, as the logic governing the system is no longer capable of ensuring the mere survival of a half of humanity. Capitalism is becoming barbarism and directly leading to genocide. More than ever, it must be replaced with different tendencies of development and a higher rationality.

Those who defend capitalism argue that the agrarian question in Europe was effectively solved through the drift from the land, and that one or two centuries later there is no reason why the countries of the South should not reproduce a similar model of change. What this forgets, however, is that the industries and urban services of nineteenth-century Europe required an abundant supply of labour, and that the surplus was able to emigrate en masse to the Americas. The contemporary third world does not have that possibility: if it wants to be competitive, as others instruct it to be, then it has to introduce modern technologies that require little labour. The polarization generated by the global expansion of capital does not allow the South to reproduce the model of the North.

So, what is to be done?

It is necessary to accept that peasant agriculture will remain throughout the foreseeable future in the twenty-first century: not out of any romantic nostalgia for the past, but quite simply because a solution to the problem must overcome the inherent tendencies of capitalism and insert itself into the long transition to world socialism. Policies must therefore be devised to regulate relations between 'the market' and peasant agriculture. At the level of individual countries and regions, a series of regulations adapted to local conditions must protect national production and ensure national food security (thus denying imperialism the use of food as a weapon), but also enable controlled population transfers from the countryside to the town through slow but steady advances in the productivity of peasant agriculture. Of course, the combination of modern industrialization with the development of peasant agriculture can and should be promoted through imaginative social policies freed from the high-waste model of core capitalism, which could anyway scarcely be generalized to ten or more billion human beings.

Far from being already solved, the 'agrarian question' is more than ever at the heart of the challenges facing humanity in the twenty-first century. The answers that are given to it will decisively shape the future course of history.

In this respect China has one major trump card (the legacy of its revolution), which could allow it to provide one possible model of what needs to be done. For access to the land must be recognized as a basic right for half of humanity, without which it will not have the conditions for survival. This right is ignored by capitalism; it does not even get a mention in the UN Charter of Rights. But it is still today recognized in China (and Vietnam). The supreme illusion would be to imagine that, by discarding that right and making land a commodity (as all the capitalist propagandists in China are proposing), it would be possible to 'speed up the modernization process'.

The modernization of agriculture was certainly one of the four modernizations formulated by Zhou Enlai. This in no way entails, how-ever, that higher agricultural output requires restricting access to the land to a small minority. Such a course would doubtless yield sharp rises in output for some, but only at the price of stagnation for the many. Indeed there is a great risk that, for the average peasant who remains on the land or migrates to the shantytowns, the agricultural growth would ultimately bear very meagre results. This is not the kind of hard fact that is of interest to the unconditional supporters of capitalism. Accumulation and enrichment of the few are the only law it knows; the exclusion of 'unproductive' sectors of the population – billions of human beings – is not its problem.

The history of China over the last half-century has shown that another road – one that respects the right of all to the land and seeks to involve the whole peasantry in the modernization process – can yield favourable results in comparison with the capitalist road. (A contrast with India is highly instructive in the respect.) It certainly should not be seen as an 'easy option', for the strategies, institutions and forms of intervention that give it the greatest desirable effectiveness are not the same everywhere (in all regions of China) and at all stages of evolution. The error of the Soviet kolkhoz model or the Chinese communes was precisely that, in parallel with central planning, they erected their particular formula into a once-and-for-all solution. My own position coincides with that of many Chinese peasant organizations and William Hinton, who advocate for the present stage a policy of support for various kinds of voluntary co-operatives.

Whether one likes it or not, the 'agrarian question' remains one of the central issues in the challenge of modernization. The core–periphery opposition is itself largely produced and reproduced by the 'capitalist road' option, whose effects on societies in the periphery have been and continue to be disastrous. The 'peasant road', combined with other elements of a 'market socialist' stage, is the only adequate response in principle, the only one capable of lifting third world societies out of their 'underdevelopment' and the extreme poverty that afflicts billions of human beings, as well as ending the situation in which their states play an insignificant role in the world arena.

5. The legacy of the Chinese Revolution will continue to carry considerable positive weight. The achievements of the last twenty years – exceptional levels of balanced economic growth, massive and generally successful urbanization (200 million new town dwellers), a remarkable capacity for the absorption of new technology – are often described as miraculous, but in fact they are not. They could not have happened without the revolution that paved the way for them. This judgement, which I share with nearly all creditable Chinese intellectuals, has been developed in my previous writings on China. Only propagandists of American imperialism, and their European or Chinese imitators, pretend that things stand differently. China's often debated shortcomings – social and regional inequalities, unemployment, rural depopulation – are in no way comparable to the catastrophes seen elsewhere in the capitalist third world, whether their experiences are also described as 'miraculous' (though having no future) or given some other epithet. The Chinese are largely unaware of such realities and therefore underestimate their own successes, but anyone familiar with the third world cannot be blind to the huge differences with the other peripheries of the global system.

'China is a poor country where you see few poor people.' China feeds 22 per cent of the world's population, although it has only 6 per cent of its arable land. That is the real miracle. It would be wrong to explain this mainly in terms of the antiquity of Chinese civilization. For, although it is true that until the Industrial Revolution China was generally more advanced in technological terms than any other major region in the world, its situation deteriorated in the course of a century and a half and produced a spectacle of widespread poverty comparable to that of India and other peripheral countries ravaged by imperialist expansion. China owes its remarkable recovery to its revolution. Brazil, by contrast, lies at the other end of the spectrum created by global capitalist expansion: 'a rich country where you see nothing but poor people'.

Few third world countries are as poor as China, in terms of the relationship between population and arable surface; to my knowledge, only Vietnam, Bangladesh and Egypt are as badly off. Some parts of India and Java are in comparable straits, but not India or Indonesia as a whole. Yet in India, Egypt and Bangladesh, as in nearly the whole of Latin America (with the exception of Cuba), the spectacle of boundless poverty immediately strikes any honest observer. No one in good faith who has travelled thousands of miles through the rich and poor regions of China, and visited many of its large cities, can fail to admit that he never encountered there anything as shaming as the unavoidable sights in the countryside and shantytowns of the third world. There cannot be the slightest doubt that the reason for China's success is its radical peasant revolution and the equal access to the land that it guaranteed.

The revolution brought Chinese society into the modern world. Its modernity, in the sense of a cultural break through which citizens consider themselves responsible for their own history, is expressed in all aspects of behaviour, although it is an incomplete modernity, as in any other country where it dominates people's thinking, ideologies and conduct. This modernity explains why one does not see in China any expression of the para-cultural neuroses that plague the Muslim countries, Hindu India or sub-Saharan Africa. The Chinese lead the life of their times: they do not live on those forms of nostalgia for a mythological past which elsewhere are the dominant background music. They do not experience any 'identity problem'.

Now, although modernity does not automatically produce democracy, it does create the conditions for it. Democracy is unthinkable without modernity. Comparatively few countries in the periphery of the capitalist system have made this leap into modernity (Korea and Taiwan, in this respect and others, are exceptions for which I will not here examine the deeper reasons). Indeed, the current period is generally marked by terrible regression at this level, through which the failure of capitalism expresses itself. 'The old world is dying, the new is not yet born, and in this half-light all manner of monsters proliferate', Gramsci had already written. In this connection, the dominant discourse concerning cultural legacies supposedly favourable or unfavourable to democracy does nothing other than sow further confusion. For, in attributing unvarying transhistorical characteristics to certain 'cultures', it pays no heed to the break that comes with modernity. The modernity into which China has enthusiastically thrown itself provides a major asset for the future. I do not know whether it will generate rapidly enough a popular aspiration to democracy and the invention of appropriate forms. But that is not impossible, and the outcome will largely depend on the ways in which democratic and social struggles are linked together.

Revolution and the plunge into modernity have transformed the Chinese people more than any other in the contemporary third world: the popular classes are self-confident, know how to fight and realize that struggle pays; they have largely shaken off the attitudes of submission that are such a mournful presence in so many other countries. Equality has become an essential value in the common ideology, as it is in France (which also had a great revolution) but not in the United States. All these profound changes are expressed in a remarkable assertiveness. Social struggles take place every day by the thousand, often in violent forms, and do not always end in defeat. The regime knows this, and uses repression (a ban on autonomous organization by the popular classes) to prevent struggles from going beyond a local horizon and to draw their sting through the art of 'dialogue' and manipulation. Nor are such struggles fortunate enough to please most of the Western champions of 'human rights', who are not interested in, and in some cases feel positively uneasy about, democracy in the service of class struggle. On the other hand, the democratic demands that they all systematically uphold are those put forward by the 'liberals', whose virulent defence of the virtues of capitalism is another phenomenon that the regime seeks to tone down.

6. The national question also occupies a central place in Chinese debates, and in the political struggles between supporters of different evolutionary paths.

From 1840 to 1949 China was the victim of constant imperialist aggression by the Western powers and Japan, as were all the nations of Asia and Africa. The aggressors knew how to forge alliances with reactionary ruling classes in China – 'feudal classes', 'compradors' (a word first coined by the Chinese Communists) and warlords. The liberation war led by the Communist Party gave China back its dignity and rebuilt its unity, the Taiwan issue now being the only one still unresolved. All Chinese people know this.

And, in spite of the regionalism inevitable in a country of this size, one cannot but feel glad that the Chinese (Han) nation is a reality. The only national questions that are handled in a debatable manner are those concerning the Tibetans and the Uighurs. (I do not at all share the point of view of those 'defenders of democracy' who sing the praises of, and place themselves at the service of, the lamas and mullahs – forces which, apart from their obscurantism, always exploited their own peoples with barbaric violence, until the Chinese Revolution came and set them free.) Imperialism actively sets out to turn these weaknesses of the regime to its advantage.

I shall go a little further in giving voice to my intuitions. I have had the opportunity to discuss the most varied issues with middle-ranking leaders of all kinds in China, though not with many higher up. My feeling, perhaps based on overgeneralization, is that those involved in economic management tend to be on the right, while those in charge of politics remain lucid about what in my view is a fundamental point: they generally consider Washington's hegemonism to be the number one enemy of China (as a nation and a state, not only because it is 'social-ist'). They say this often, and are fairly straightforward about it. In this respect, I am still struck by the difference between their language and that which Soviet (or a fortiori East European) political leaders used with apparent conviction. For the latter always seemed to me completely unaware of the real aims of Washington and its subordinate Western allies. The kind of speech that Gorbachev made in Reykjavik in 1985 – when he proclaimed with incredible naivety that the hostility of the United States towards the USSR had 'ended' – would be unthinkable in China. As chance had it, I discussed that speech in Beijing shortly after it was made, and all the Chinese were dumbfounded by its stupidity. They grew heated and did not hesitate to say that the United States was and would remain their enemy, their main enemy.

The Chinese are strongly conscious of their country's place in history. Its very name in Chinese – Chung Kuo – does not refer to a particular ethnicity; it simply means 'Middle Empire' (and People's Republic of China reads in Chinese as 'People's Republic of the Middle Empire'). The decline of their nation was felt by them to be intolerable. This is why the Chinese intelligentsia always turned to those external 'models' which, in its view, would allow it to discover what it had to do to give China its rightful place in the modern world. After 4 May 1919 the model was either Japan (which inspired the Kuomintang) or revolutionary Russia (the one that finally carried the day, because it associated the struggle against imperialism with revolutionary social change involving the whole people). With Japan in crisis, Russia in a state of collapse and Europe itself striving to imitate the United States, there is a danger that China will no longer see modernity and progress except through the 'American model' – even though it is the model of their enemy, as Japan was before. China, a great nation, always compares itself to the most powerful.

I do not wish to underestimate the dangers implicit in this way of looking at things, and in the illusion of 'American friendship' that it fosters in the younger generation. For it tends to obscure the fact that the rebuilding of internationalism among the world's peoples is of crucial importance in rolling back the aggressive hegemonism of the United States. Behind the European ruling classes, whose strategic alignment with Washington is intended solely to defend the joint interests of dominant capital within the collective triad imperialism, there are peoples whose vision of modernity differs from the one that globalized and Americanized neoliberalism seeks to impose. Behind the hard-pressed comprador regimes in the third world, there are peoples that rolled back an earlier imperialism through the Afro-Asian solidarity expressed in the Non-Aligned Movement. As to China, it gained huge popularity at the time as a result of its construction of the Tanzania–Zambia (Tanzam) railway (the only major initiative that freed southern Africa from its physical dependence on the apartheid regime in South Africa), and as a result of the activity of Chinese doctors in the remotest villages of Africa. To revive the solidarity of the Asian and African peoples in the face of the savage aggression of US hegemonism is one of the chief tasks of the anti-imperialist strategy that is called for today and in the years to come. This is a necessity for China and for all the other countries. It is the precondition if the Saddam Husseins and bin Ladens of this world are no longer to occupy centre stage in the resistance to imperialism.

7. There is no reason to be surprised that all the great revolutions in history were followed by reversals, 'restorations' or 'counter-revolutions'.

But, although these set things straight again, they did not succeed in destroying the fertile seeds of a nobler revolutionary vision. Only the minor revolutions – if that term is appropriate to them – such as England's (inglorious) Glorious Revolution of 1688 or the so-called American Revolution that changed nothing in the colonial social system but merely transferred political power from the metropolis to the settlers: only these can boast of '100 per cent success', because they did little more than register what was occurring spontaneously in society.

Yet reversal is always a serious matter. It threatens Russia with virtual disappearance as a nation, and there are no visible signs yet that it will be able to pull itself together. It threatens China with becoming stuck in a peripheral capitalism without a future – and a list of the negative phenomena already expressing this danger would not be hard to compile. The new Chinese bourgeoisie is no less coarse and egoistic than the comprador bourgeoisies of the contemporary third world. It does not (or not yet) occupy the centre of the political stage, but it certainly has the means to organize corruption and other ways of influencing decisions. Young members of the booming new middle class display the same spectacle of 'Americanization', no doubt superficial in its immediate appearances but concealing a profound depoliticization. Young workers used to be sent to the Soviet Union to learn to make aircraft engines. The children of the new middle class go to the United States to learn hotel management.

An uncertain future

Under these conditions, the future of China remains uncertain: the battle for socialism has not been won there. But nor has it yet been lost. In my view, it will not be lost until the day when the Chinese system revokes the right of all its peasants to the land – until then, political and social struggles will still be capable of affecting the course of development. The ruling political class uses the instruments of its bureaucratic dictatorship to suppress such struggles, and sections of this class think they can use the same means to prevent the rise of the bourgeoisie. The bourgeoisie and middle classes as a whole are not determined to fight for democracy and have no difficulty accepting the model of 'Asian-style' autocracy, so long as it gives the green light to their consumer appetites. The popular classes, for their part, are fighting to defend their economic and social rights. Will they manage to unify their struggles, to invent adequate forms of struggle, to formulate a positive alternative programme, to define the content and the means of a democracy that can be of service to them?

Three sets of scenarios may be envisaged around which the future may be built. These three schemas correspond to: (i) the imperialist project of dismembering the country and compradorizing its coastal regions; (ii) a project of 'national' capitalist development; and (iii) a project of national popular development that combines, in a manner both complementary and conflictual, capitalist market tendencies and social tendencies forming part of a long-term socialist perspective (of which the project would be the next phase in the years to come).

The option in favour of a deregulated market and maximum openness – the one supported by Chinese and foreign liberals – plays into the hands of imperialist strategy, for it heightens the depoliticization and silent opposition of the popular classes at the same time that it increases the external vulnerability of the Chinese nation and state. Evidently this option does not bring any promise of democratization, nor would it raise China from its status as a dominated peripheral participant forced to play by the rules of the new triad imperialism. What distinguishes the third model from the second might at first seem hard to pinpoint with any precision: namely, control over external relations, together with modes of redistribution that maintain an acceptable level of social and regional solidarity. But in fact it is not just a question of how powerful are the instruments of state policy; the difference lies in the very nature of the two models. It is here that the real debate has its ultimate basis. The progressive option can set no other priority than an expansion of the internal market, on the basis of social relations regulated in such a way as to reduce social and regional inequalities to the maximum possible degree; hence external relations are subordinated to this driving logic. The other, contrasting option takes ever deeper insertion into the world capitalist system as the main driving force of economic development; it is an option inevitably associated with worsening regional and social inequalities. Expressed in these terms, the alternative leaves but little room for a 'national capitalism' capable of eventually catching up the developed capitalist world and making China a new great power, or even a superpower that forces the existing powers to abandon their hegemonism. It is unlikely that any political regime could hold its course for long within this narrow room for manoeuvre, and therefore that a strategy inspired by this perspective could avoid falling either to the right (by eventually submitting to the imperialist project) or to the left (by evolving towards the third model).

3

Russia out of the tunnel?

In an article, 'La Russie dans le système mondial: géographie ou histoire?' (republished in *Les Défis de la mondialisation*, 1996), I offered my vision of the place that the Eurasian space (with borders from Poland to China) occupied in successive stages of the formation of the global system and in this context defined the challenges faced by the Russian Empire and subsequently the USSR. Here I propose to focus on the challenges which post-Soviet Russia has faced since that time. However great the transformations that have taken place in Russia over the course of the last fifteen years may appear, they are not 'revolutionary' (or 'counter-revolutionary'); they are the result of the acceleration of underlying trends that were already in existence within the Soviet system in the 1930s and have been gathering force since then.

I will not limit myself on this subject to stating that Soviet society at that time was not (or no longer) 'socialist', as the promoters of the 1917 revolution wanted, but was a specific type of capitalism (which I described as 'capitalism without capitalists') destined to become 'normal' capitalism (i.e. capitalism with capitalists), which is indeed the plan of the new ruling class (which sprang from the preceding class, no less) even though, as we shall see, the reality of the system that it has put in place falls far short of this plan. I will go further by proposing an analysis of the characteristics of the Soviet system (as a social system, a power system and a method of integration into the global system) and their continued existence in deteriorated forms in Russia today.

Basic characteristics of the Soviet system

I define the Soviet system through five basic characteristics: corporatism, autocratic power, social stabilization, economic delinking from the global capitalist system, and integration into this system as a superpower. The concept of 'totalitarian regime', popularized by the dominant ideological discourse, is shown here as elsewhere to be flat and hollow, incapable of taking account of Soviet reality, its methods of management and the contradictions that led to the evolution and transformation under way.

For the purposes of the analysis that follows, I have retained those noteworthy characteristics which appear to me to sum up the essential nature of what the Soviet system became in its last, Brezhnevite, phase. The revolution of 1917 was a grand revolutionary transition in human history. It held out a rich and much needed promise. The object of this chapter is not to rewrite its history in order to abolish its importance, even if it is fashionable these days to do that, still less to give the impression that these leading characteristics highlighted in this chapter had already been contained in the revolution, or in Leninism, or even Stalinism. My decision in how to characterize it has the sole purpose of clarifying the nature of what followed and the challenges that it now throws up for the survival of the people of the former Soviet Union.

A corporatist regime

By corporatist regime I mean that the working class (supposed to become 'ruling' class) had lost its unifying political consciousness both through the action of the policies put in place by those in power and through the objective conditions of the rapid mushrooming of their number during accelerated industrialization. The workers of each enterprise, or group of enterprises forming a 'combinat', together with their management and directors, constituted a social/economic 'bloc' and defended their place within the system. These 'blocs' confronted each other on all levels: in negotiations (bargaining) between ministries and departments of Gosplan and in daily dealings with enterprises from combinats other than their own. The unions, reduced to work management (work and employment conditions) and the social benefits of the workers concerned, found their natural place in this corporatist system.

The corporatism in question had a crucial role to play in the reproduction and expansion of the system as a whole. It involved a double substitution: (i) of the principle of 'profitability' that in the last resort governs decisions to invest in capitalism, and (ii) of the market that in capitalism still defines the way in which prices are determined. Corporatism constituted the reality that 'planning' hid through its intentions to gain acceptance for a 'so-called scientific rationale' of the macro-economic management of the production system.

Corporatism emphasized the regionalist dimension in the negotiations/ bargaining between competing blocs. This regionalism was not based on the principle of 'national' diversity (as in Tito's federal Yugoslavia). The relationship between Russia – the dominant nation both numerically and historically – and other nations was not a 'colonial' one. The redistribution of investment and social benefits that operated to the detriment of the 'Russians' and to the benefit of the peripheral regions bear this out. In this regard, I do not accept the nonsense of comparing the USSR to an 'imperial' system dominating its 'internal colonies' in spite of the impression of the 'dominance' of the Russian nation (and even the arrogance of some of its expressions). Perhaps the Baltic States will learn that they have exchanged an advantageous position from which they benefited as part of the USSR for a subjugated position within the European Union. The Caucasians and the peoples of central Asia will be brutally dealt with as colonies by the Westerners, having lost the bargaining power that they enjoyed within the USSR. The regionalism in question concerned small regions (within the republics to which they belonged) with common interests to defend in a global system that ensured their independence, which was in fact always more unequal than Gosplan's rationalizing discourse claimed.

Autocratic power

The choice of the term is not intended to weaken the critique of the system; in the case of 'the absence of democracy' it is easy to see whether we are talking of representative forms (elections there brought no surprises) or participation as envisaged by the revolutionaries of 1917. For the unions and every other social organization were subjected to central state control, which effectively precluded participation in decision-making at any level.

Yet this fact provides no explanation of the pseudo-concept of 'totalitarianism'. Autocratic power was disputed within the ruling class – the representatives of the corporate blocs. What to outward appearances was an autocracy masked the reality of a power that rested on the 'peaceful' resolution of corporatist conflicts through consideration for one another.

Here again, the autocratic management of the conflicts in question necessarily took on regional dimensions. The structure of the system comprised a pyramid of powers that fitted together ranging from management (always autocratic) of local interests to those of the Union and the republics. This regional dimension, sometimes but not necessarily 'ethnic', facilitated the break-up of the Union and the threatened break-up of the republics (Russia first), which is today a dangerous challenge for the central powers.

Stabilized social order

It is not my intention to ignore the extreme violence that accompanied the building of the Soviet system. These violent acts were of different kinds. The major conflict pitted the defenders of the socialist plan at the origin of the revolution against 'realists' who, in practice if not in their rhetoric, gave absolute priority to 'catching up' through accelerated industrialization–modernization. This conflict was the inevitable result of the objective contradiction that the revolution faced. It was necessary to 'catch up' (or at least reduce the gap) as the revolution inherited a 'backward' country (I find the expression 'peripheral capitalism' preferable), and simultaneously to build 'something else' (socialism). I have stressed this contradiction, which I have placed at the heart of the problems related with overcoming capitalism on a world scale (the 'long transition from capitalism to global socialism'), and will not return to it here. Communist militants were themselves the main victims of this first major contradiction underlying the violence of the regime.

A second type of violence accompanied accelerated industrialization. Some aspects of this can be compared to the type of violence that accompanied the construction of capitalism in the West, the massive migration from the countryside to the towns and the wretched circumstances associated with proletarianization (overcrowded accommodation etc.). The fact remains that the USSR carried out this construction in record time

– a few decades – compared with the entire century it took in central capitalist countries. The latter benefited from the extra advantages of their dominant imperialist positions and the option of allowing their 'surplus' population to emigrate to the Americas. The violence of the primitive accumulation in the USSR is, in this respect, no more tragic than it was elsewhere. On the contrary, no doubt, for the accelerated industrialization in the USSR allowed the children of the popular classes to benefit from massive social mobility unknown in the systems of the countries of central capitalism dominated by the bourgeoisie. In spite of everything else, it is this 'specificity' inherited from original socialist intentions that won the majority of the working classes and even 'collectivized' peasantry over to the system, even if it was autocratic.

Furthermore, let us not forget the violence committed by the dominant global capitalist system: military intervention, most savage in the Nazi aggression, and economic blockades.

The Soviet system, however contradictory it may have been, succeeded in building a social order capable of stability, and which was in fact stable during its post-Stalin period. Social peace was 'bought' by moderation in the exercise of power (although still autocratic), the improvement of material conditions and tolerance of 'illegal' discrepancies. Certainly, stability of this kind is not destined to last 'eternally', but no system is, in spite of the claims made by ideological discourse (be it 'socialist' or that of capitalist 'liberalism'). Soviet stability masked the contradictions and limitations of the system, which summed up its difficulty in passing from extensive to intensive forms of accumulation, like its difficulty in emerging from autocracy and allowing the democratization of its political management. Yet this contradiction might have found a solution in an 'evolution' towards what I have described as the 'centre left': the opening up of market spaces (without challenging the dominant forms of collective property) and democratization. Perhaps this was the intention of Gorbachev, whose failed attempt – naive in many ways – brought down the regime 'on the right' from 1990 onwards.

Economic delinking of the Soviet System

For the most part, the Soviet production system was effectively delinked from the dominant global capitalist system. I mean by this that the rationale that governed the economic decisions of those in power (investments and pricing) did not derive from demands for 'open' integration into globalization. It is thanks to this disconnection that the system succeeded in progressing as swiftly as it did.

This system was not, however, 'wholly' independent of the 'rest of the (capitalist) world'. No system can be and delinking, in my definition of the concept, is not a synonym of 'autarky'. Through its integration into the global system, the USSR occupied a 'peripheral' position, mainly as an exporter of raw materials.

A military and political superpower

Through the success rather than the failure of its construction, the USSR succeeded in working its way up to the rank of military superpower. It was the Soviet army that defeated the Nazis, and then, after the war, succeeded in record time in ending the United States' nuclear and conventional weapons monopoly. These successes are at the origin of its political presence on the post-war world scene. In addition, the Soviet regime gained considerable prestige from its victory over Nazi Germany, and from the construction of what it claimed, however illusorily, to be socialism (sometimes called 'actually existing socialism'). Contrary to the assertions of anti-Soviet propaganda, it made 'moderate' use of this prestige: it did not set out to 'export the revolution' or to 'conquer' western Europe (the spurious motive used by Washington and the European bourgeoisies to get Nato accepted). It did, however, use its political (and military) might to compel dominant imperialism to pull back from the third world, opening up a margin of autonomy for the dominant classes (and the peoples) of Asia and Africa, which they lost with the fall of the USSR. It is not by chance that the United States' hegemonic military offensive developed with the violence we have witnessed from 1990 onwards. The Soviet presence from 1945 to 1990 imposed a 'multipolar' organization on the world.

New forms of capitalism in Russia

The title of this section deliberately avoids the term 'neoliberalism', which – though I sometimes use it like everyone else because it has been imposed by the dominant discourse – actually involves ideological rhetoric that hinders serious thinking.

'Neoliberalism', or more generally liberalism, will be called into question both in the West and in the East, when its failure is recognized. In fact 'liberalism' is to 'actually existing capitalism' what 'socialist' discourse was to 'actually existing socialism': an ideological tool designed to eliminate the analysis of real questions. 'Liberalism' promises everything at once: 'efficiency' (without defining the term), 'democracy', 'peace' and even social justice! But the policies implemented in its name produce almost the opposite: stagnation (and in some cases even decline), the deterioration of democracy (or even the reinforcement of autocracies), permanent war and increasing inequality. Yet it matters little, we are asked to 'wait'...

The collapse of the Soviet system, reinforced by that of the populism of the third world and the erosion of the social-democratic commitment in the West, has allowed so-called liberal ideology to triumph and led to vast support for its discourse. This is true in Russia as elsewhere. Incidentally, I have pointed out the illusion entertained according to which, just as Germany and Japan had 'lost the war but won the peace', Russia would, thanks to liberalism, undertake accelerated and (finally) effective modernization and development of democracy. We forget – or pretend to forget – that Washington's objective is not to allow the rebirth of a strong Russia (any more than that of a strong China), even if capitalist, but to destroy it.

Have fifteen years of 'reforms' culminated in the setting up in Russia of a capitalist system capable of 'stabilizing' the country and thereafter of putting it effectively on the path of liberal promises? Reality obliges us to answer no: the USSR has disintegrated and in turn Russia lives under the threat of disintegration, none of the institutions in place (its private enterprises or its state) is equipped to carry out the necessary investments to improve the efficiency of the production system (on the contrary, disinvestment is massive), and the systematic destruction of the Soviet system's positive achievements (education in particular) does not point to a 'brighter future'. It is difficult to see how a system with these characteristics could 'stabilize', except temporarily on the basis of complete impoverishment and powerlessness.

So, in fact, these new forms of capitalism in Russia have increased rather than reduced the characteristics of a Soviet system in advanced decline.

Russia on the periphery of the imperialist capitalist system

'Open' Russia is not only an 'exporter of raw materials' (oil first and foremost), it is liable to become no more than that. Its industrial and agricultural production systems no longer benefit from the attention of the authorities and are of interest to neither the national private sector nor foreign capital. There has been no investment worthy of the name to make their progress possible and they only survive at the expense of the continued deterioration of their infrastructure. The capacity for technological renewal and the high-quality education that underpinned it in the Soviet system is being systematically destroyed.

Who is responsible for these massive declines? First, of course, the new ruling class, which for the most part originated from the former Soviet ruling class, made fabulously rich, no doubt, through the privatization/ pillage from which it has benefited. The concentration of this new class has, moreover, reached uncommon proportions, to the extent that the term 'oligarchy' suits them perfectly. The similarity with the oligarchies of Latin America is certainly striking. This class owes its increasing wealth to three sources: income from oil (which depends on world cir-cumstances– that is, high or low prices of crude), the cannibalization of industries (privatized industrial firms are not destined to form the basis of increased and more efficient production but only to allow the oligarchies to survive through their decline), and commission from opening the country's markets up to imports. Income from oil rents plus commissions defines a comprador bourgeoisie, not a 'national' bourgeoisie.

Imperialism benefits from and supports the country's decline to the rank of minor periphery. Essentially, so far as Russia and other former USSR republics are concerned, the United States plans to reduce them to the rank of minor deindustrialized and therefore powerless peripheries: in other words, to 'Latin-Americanize' the former Soviet East (the former USSR and Eastern Europe). The methods are designed in varying propor-tions depending on the case, ranging from total destruction for countries with a revolutionary past (Russia and Yugoslavia) to a milder form of subordination in 'conservative' Eastern Europe (Poland, Hungary, etc.).

Of course, in the context of this common vision shared by the powers that be in the United States and in Europe, a certain competition may appear among the various associates of the imperialist triad. Who has most to gain from this Latin-Americanization? The United States or (western) Europe? The current compromise leaves eastern Europe mainly to Germany, and Russia to the United States. Nato (under the preponderant influence of the United States), the WTO and Brussels (whose liberal options only serve to strengthen those of the WTO) are entrusted with the task of 'managing' this essentially asymmetrical system. The fact remains that the management of the political responsibilities of collective imperialism is riddled with contradictions which I have analysed elsewhere and which I will not go into again here. European/United States rivalry is at work in the context of this management and in this respect Washington has several cards to play which cannot be ignored. These include, obviously, London's unwavering Atlanticist inclination and also that of the servile political classes of eastern Europe. Europe missed the opportunity to build a rapprochement with Russia that would have ensured its autonomy vis-à-vis the hegemonic attitude of the USA.

The oligarchy's explosion of wealth has led to the formation of a new 'middle class' known as the 'new Russians'. The jobs these people hold are entirely unproductive, having derived from the oligarchs' spending, whereas the former middle class, made up of professionals and engineers who were in general far more highly qualified and certainly more productive, have ended up with the popular classes and among the victims of this comprador capitalist development. Moreover, the monopolistic oligarchies, the exclusive beneficiaries of state generosity, make the formation of a class of authentic and inventive entrepreneurs impossible. They are persecuted by mafias and the state itself, rendering the appearance of capitalism from below impossible.

The liberal discourse according to which the 'winners' of the system are the most highly qualified and inventive individuals while the 'losers' are the 'least productive' workers does not stand up to serious examination. In actual fact, the 'losers' are all those working in production in the new Russia.

Irresponsible autocratic power

The capitalist forms of the new Russia exclude all democratic progress. Autocracy is no longer a 'vestige of the past' here but a necessary form of existence of the comprador oligarchy's power. The new constitution of

1993 established, to serve it, a presidential regime that reduces the powers of the Duma (elected parliament) to nothing. As we know, western governments pretend to ignore it, saving their reproaches for the democratic deficit in the only regimes that resist liberalism while they approve the dictatorship of those that serve it.

The distinguishing feature of the new autocracy as compared with the former one lies elsewhere, namely in the totally irresponsible character of the power that it exerts. The autocracy is at the service of the oligarchy and takes part in the battles that the clans are engaged in even though it knows how to ensure it is paid for services rendered. In fact, this autocracy has placed itself at the service of globalized oligopolistic foreign capital which it facilitates without the slightest resistance from the diktats issued by the WTO, the IMF and even Nato!

The conflicts that recently pitted Putin against certain oligarchs have not brought about significant change in the organization of the system. Putin's objectives remained limited: first of all, to strengthen the positions of the clan of the St Petersburg oligarchs (the new president's client base) to the detriment of the others, then – perhaps – to 'rationalize' the system by separating more distinctly autocratic presidential state bureaucracy from the class that it has never renounced serving. Each has his role but all are part of the same play.

Are the 'Russian people' responsible for this decline? Certainly to some extent, through the utter confusion they find themselves in following the brutal collapse of the Soviet institutions (sometimes destroyed by cannon fire, as was the case with the first elected parliament!). The new political parties had no social or ideological basis that would have allowed them to emerge from their nonexistence. The new 'right', reduced in fact to individual irresponsible cliques originating from the former system, have certainly successfully handled demagogic rhetoric amplified by the corrupt media at their service. Their stories are no less rapidly used, faced with a generally shrewd public opinion that is evidence of the considerable politicization of the Russian people. Because of this, the new right rapidly found itself captive of the bureaucratic power of the new autocracy. The fact remains that the Communist Party, in spite of the hopes placed in it by a large minority of the electorate (nearly 50 per cent), did not know how to reinvent itself (and move away from its legacy of the autocratic administration of power) or even resist the pressure of the new dictatorship. On the contrary, it has facilitated its establishment by subscribing to the new constitution. It then tried to make people forget its stupid cowardice and the major errors that it made by initiating ambiguous 'nationalist' discourse. Yet the embryonic political parties of the alternative left have not proved their capacity to undermine the plans of the new oligarchy and are rapidly withdrawing into intellectual cliques isolated from the popular classes.

Degenerated and weakened corporatism

Faced with the obtuse and declining Communist Party, the trade unions could have provided an effective pole of resistance as they have retained the respect and support of their members, who number in the millions, for at least twelve years.

The major error made by trade union leaders was to think that the former corporatism that enveloped them could guarantee their 'survival'. It is true that the objective situation facilitated this error of judgement and perspective. In the great majority of cases, directors and people in managerial positions in the enterprises excluded from the new system of oligarchic powers remained 'on the side of their workers' in the daily fight for the survival of production. For their part, some social-democratic ideologists cherished the illusion that the establishment of the tripartite arrangement that they recommended (employer, union, state) allowed a kind of positive 'historical compromise'. These ideologists were a war too late – social democracy in the West having announced its conversion to liberalism – and were not sufficiently aware that the model of peripheral capitalism under construction in Russia excluded all 'social' forms of managing it.

The cowardice of the trade union leadership and the illusions that they were under did not prevent social struggles from breaking out here and there (numerous strikes) and sometimes the regime was forced to retreat, as was the case with the threat to bring the country to a halt through the resistance of the railway workers. However, these struggles did not succeed in bringing about much needed reviews in the methods of trade union management, and the attempts of a few groups from the 'new left' to re-establish working-class life on independent and new union bases achieved no more than anecdotal success.

This combination of unfavourable factors sowed the seeds of the decline of the trade union movement discernible over recent years. The collapse of the social services that the trades unions managed under the Soviet system has, for its part, contributed to this disaffection.

Uncontrolled regionalism

The strong regionalism of ageing Sovietism has entered a phase of destructive decline. Regionalism was formerly controlled, not necessarily by state violence but rather by the need for the Soviet autocracy to accept the necessary compromises.

The clans of the new irresponsible autocracy think, on the contrary, that it is useful to exploit regionalism to serve their short-term objectives. In some cases this adverse trend has gone very far, as is borne out by the Chechen situation.

That there were serious questions waiting to be answered in certain regions, especially in the 'non-Russian' areas of the Russian Federation, cannot be ignored. No one can doubt that 'external forces' tried to exploit these difficulties, including of course the United States and its Islamic allies in the case of Chechnya. However, Moscow is responsible for the deterioration of the situation. A large majority of the Chechen people rejected the appeals by the 'Islamists' for secession. Those in power in Russia refused the support of this majority and deliberately opted to play the 'military intervention' card with scant regard for the consequences of this decision. Clearly this was the product of expedient calculations on the part of the clans of the oligarchy (interested, for example, in the route of the oil line from the Caspian Sea) and the state bureaucracy (rebuild 'the unity of the Russian people' and obtain their 'unconditional' support in the face of 'the external terrorist enemy').

It is known that the terrorist attacks in Moscow and elsewhere, which have not been proved to be the work of Chechens, have fulfilled similar functions to 11 September, exploited as we know by the Bush administration.

In this respect, too, Putin's administration does not seem to have broken with the errors made by Yeltsin. The second Chechen war, undertaken by Putin, resulted in the same failure as the first and has been 'exploited' in the same way by the two successive presidents. Putin can be credited with a reform of the territorial organization of the powers designed to put an end to regionalist flare-ups. The fact remains that this reform is still governed by the principle of autocracy (doubling the elected governors by a kind of appointed prefects) and refuses to rely on the populations concerned (which would risk strengthening their capacity for resistance to the pressure exerted by the oligarchs). The reform undertaken is therefore not likely to favour the right solution for open or latent conflicts.

Russia removed from the international scene

Since then Russia has held a minor position in the G7, now the G8 (G7½). Yet for all that it is not an active player in the maintenance of global balance. To all appearances, it preserves considerable military power, second in the world in terms of its nuclear equipment and conventional missiles although the deterioration of its military organization gives reason to fear that it may be incapable of using this arsenal effectively, were it necessary, which is to say in the event of US aggression.

It goes without saying that this effacement poses a problem for the future of the global system. Which 'camp' will Russia eventually settle in, in the event that political differences between certain European countries (France and Germany) on the one hand and the United States on the other succeed in shattering the Atlanticism that is still in command of the collective imperialism of the triad, or if the conflict with certain Southern countries (China, or even India, Iran or North Korea) were to grow? Certainly in the short term, the question does not arise: Europe remains Atlanticist in spite of the gnashing of teeth by a certain few. Even if Russia were to align itself, like China, with France and Germany in order not to give Washington carte blanche in its aggression in Iraq, the gesture has not brought about a 'switch of alliances'. Moscow is still hitched up to the American cart in spite of some (moderate) defiance. Washington made no mistake in that respect, reserving its violent condemnation for the French alone. The pressure exerted by the military presence of the United States in central Asia and Caucasia, their recent establishment in Georgia and their manipulation of the Islamic threats have so far managed to keep Russia out of the big international game. Russia could derail the US plan aimed at reducing its economy to the status of a minor subordinated periphery. It could do so by playing an active role in the revival of a 'southern front', in the first place by drawing closer to China. But Russia did not choose this way; rather the opposite. Russian calculations are based on the illusion that only the country's alliance with the USA can protect it from eventual Chinese expansionist ambitions in Siberia and central Asia. By doing so, Russia strengthens the chances of the US strategy aimed at isolating its major potential competitor – China. I do not believe that Russia will be rewarded for this 'service', which, on the contrary, will accelerate its decline.

Yet the fact remains that all these balances (or imbalances) which benefit the United States remain fragile and the certain failure of its intervention in Iraq will sooner or later end up calling them into question.

Will Russian diplomacy find its place in this redistribution of the cards? I will return to this question, which constitutes one of the major dimensions of the construction of an alternative to liberal American globalization.

Ideological decline

Soviet ideology continued to feed on supposedly 'socialist' rhetoric. Even severely depleted, Soviet power knew that its legitimacy lay in the Revolution of 1917. Although this was irritating and even worthy of derision, the distance that separated this rhetoric from Soviet reality was no greater than that which separated 'liberal' discourse from actually existing capitalism. Just as a good number of normal individuals support liberal discourse in spite of the social catastrophe that accompanied the reality of it, it should come as no surprise that 'socialist' discourse has had its believers up to the very last.

The new oligarchic autocracy needs to take the opposite view of Soviet discourse, but it does not know what to replace it with. Stories about economic efficiency and democracy are not credible in Russia, even though they may be in eastern Europe. 'Patriotic' discourse, therefore, constitutes the regime's last hope, now that it finally has its back against the wall. The rhetoric in question serves to remove the real problems (social inequality, the destruction of the 1917 conquests, the ineffective-ness of new economic management and the loss of international role), while pretending 'to unite the whole country behind its leaders', implying that the latter 'resist' dominant globalized capital.

I note here that this comprador bourgeois discourse closely resembles that of other ruling classes with the same type of development elsewhere, in Asia and in Africa. All comprador classes that rule contemporary peripheries try to give themselves a 'patriotic' image, although they are responsible for the decline suffered by their nations and in fact only facilitate the ('foreign') domination of international capital.

Patriotism in a positive sense is (now more than ever) certainly necessary in Russia, as it is elsewhere, faced with the challenges of American liberal globalization, so long as it is conceived of as a positive element in the construction of self-sustained development while remaining at the service of all working classes rather than becoming demagogic and deceitful rhetoric, as is the case with the discourse of the new Russian regime.

The fact remains that the ideological discourse of the new Russian regime has no real hold over its people. Evidence for this can be seen in its increasing need to resort to elections that are openly falsified on a large scale. In other words, we are dealing with a power devoid of legitimacy and credibility. Or perhaps this new Russian capitalism is incapable of finding a centre of gravity around which to stabilize its power.

The opposition's deficiency is also revealed by its ideological discourse. Communist Party leaders have rallied round the 'patriotic' discourse of the regime, barely giving it a more precise content – rather like those in Muslim countries who, 'threatened' by the wave of political Islamism, try to outbid their opponents in their chosen field in the belief that in this way they will exorcize the latter's powers of attraction. Others invoke 'Euroasianism', that is to say nationalism that is both anti-American and anti-European, and recommend a rapprochement with Asia (China, India, Iran). This rapprochement would certainly be one of the requirements for the formation of an alternative globalization. However, there is no need for dubious para-ideological legitimacy, which only distances support for modernist universalism, even if of 'Western' origin, and hence deformed by the imperialist system of which the West is the centre.

There is no doubt that serious alternative views derived from criticism of Sovietism from the left aiming to forge ahead with socialist reconstruction would find favourable ground in Russia. However, we have to understand that up to now these visions have not moved out of left intellectual circles and have no hold on the people.

Is there a worthwhile alternative in Russia today?

The picture of Russia I have portrayed in the preceding pages may seem excessively pessimistic as regards the future of the country. In fact the failure of new Russian capitalism and its inability to provide the conditions for stabilization should, on the contrary, be reason for optimism. It is sometimes said in Moscow that Russia, as on the eve of 1917, is almost ripe for a new revolution or for radical transformation capable of redressing the direction of its development. Through what local and global perspectives? Under what conditions?

The basic principles on which the alternative to the current global system should be established are simple, clear and in fact largely understood. On internal ('national') plans: (i) a 'mixed economy' that on the one hand gives the state the means to orient overall development and on the other offers private property and the market a sufficient profit margin to make the promotion of initiatives possible; (ii) the institutionalization of worker/enterprise/state collective bargaining; (iii) the development of representative democracy through the promotion of participative democracy initiatives. On a global scale: (i) the organization of the negotiation of forms of economic management (trade, capital flows, technological transfers, monetary management) based on acknowledgement of the diversity of interests and the inequality of the partners; (ii) acknowledgement of the principle of the sovereignty of the people reinforced by support for the progress of democratization, the foundations of a multipolar political world. The implementation of all of these principles would make it possible to begin an initial stage on the road to the 'long transition to world socialism'.

Of course, these very general principles, which are valid for all (China or Russia, Germany or the Congo), only come into their own when put into practice in a way that respects the diversity of objective situations.

For Russia this means: (i) the renationalization of large enterprises, particularly in oil and energy (therefore expropriation of the oligarchy);

(ii) the invention of new forms of joint management (workers and directors) of the industrial and commercial enterprises, whether these be formally public (state, communities, workers' collectives) or private; (iii) the re-establishment and reinforcement of public social services, education (which was of a high standard in the USSR) and scientific and technological research; (iv) the abolition of the constitution of 1993 and the elaboration of an authentically democratic constitution by a large elected convention; (v) support for forms of popular intervention that favour participatory democracy; (vi) the initiation of extensive negotiation between the republics of the former USSR to enable the construction of an economic and political regional space that respects the autonomy of the partners and is capable of establishing interdependence to the benefit of all; (vii) the re-establishment of Russian military power (until there is general disarmament, if the United States is ever prepared to submit to one); (viii) the development of negotiated commercial, technological and financial arrangements initiating the construction of a 'greater Europe' from the Atlantic to the Pacific; (ix) the development of a foreign policy that is active and independent (of US policy in particular), designed to strengthen the institutions responsible for the construction of a multipolar world.

From the perspective of the alternative globalization envisaged here, the place and the roles fulfilled by the national partners shall by force of circumstance remain specific and different from one another. Russia will occupy the place of both major producer/exporter of raw materials (oil and mineral products) and renewed industrial power (without being necessarily subject to the hazards that the search for 'competitiveness' on a so-called open world market implies). China's place, by comparison, is that of a new industrial power whose production would be governed principally by the enlargement of its internal market and only incidentally by its exports (the opposite of the principle that the WTO is determined to impose). This option would mean in China, as elsewhere in Asia and Africa, appropriate solutions to the agrarian problem based on acknowledgement of the right of access to land for all peasants (I refer here to what I have written elsewhere on the subject). Certainly, Russia also still has an agrarian problem (as does eastern Europe) that cannot be resolved by the development of capitalism, as it was in the developed centres of the global system. But the questions are posed here in rather different concrete terms from those that characterize the countries of the 'third world' (Asia, Africa and Latin America) and require appropriate solutions.

The government of Yevgeny Primakov had well and truly begun a recovery programme along the same lines as those described here with, it seems, plenty of determination but also considerable prudence in the initial measures taken (which is easy to understand). As Gorbachev might have wished to do but did not know how, Primakov envisaged the construction of a 'centre left' economic and political system. First, Primakov was the victim of the inability of the Communist Party (still powerful at the time) to understand and support the initiative. He was also the victim of international hostility, mainly from the United States but, unfortunately, also from Europe, which did not abandon its intention to 'Latin-Americanize' the former USSR (and also eastern Europe through the process of its integration into the European Union).

The result of this failure facilitated the initial success of the US offensive in the Middle East, central Asia and on a world scale, and reinforced the submission of Putin's regime to its immediate requirements. This fact has led Russia and the whole world to a crossroads: either American plans will be derailed (and that has become a prerequisite for the construction of an alternative on all levels, from the national to the global), or they will (for a time) continue to undermine the potential for democratization and social progress in all countries.

In this struggle, the responsibility of the people is paramount in Russia as it is elsewhere. An intensification of social struggles and democratic demands, dissipation of illusions and the beginning of the reconstruction of a new open left, capable of winning over the popular classes, which the Communist Party and the unions try to continue to treat as 'clientele' at the service of their short-term political calculations, are all positive signs of possible recovery in Russia.

Europe's responsibility is no less important. Europe must stretch out its hand to Russia. It must relinquish its self-image as a partner of the collective imperialism of the triad that is aligned with the plans of US hegemony. As I said earlier, in order to do that, it will have to find a way out of the 'quicksand' in which it has become mired.

Putin has perhaps now understood that the aim of the United States, and of Europe aligned with it, has been to destroy Russia and not to assist it in the process of renewal. But the system on which he has built his power does not allow him to stand up to the onslaught of the imperialist triad. To do that he would have to give up his support for the oligarchy which is exploiting the Russian people. The course of events in Georgia and Ukraine is an illustration of the drama. As a result of the support that the Russian authorities gave to the local satraps, whom they regarded as their friends, Moscow transformed these men's opponents into heroes, when in reality they were nothing more than vulgar agents of foreign forces. For thirty years the United States and Europe have profited from the suspicion with which the Soviet-inspired regimes in Europe have regarded democracy. This is how Lech Walesa, Washington's and the Vatican's friend, succeeded in passing himself off as the leader of a movement for Polish working-class renewal (which is how Solidarity presented itself), when his real purpose was to destroy its capacity to resist capitalism's assault. When Walesa came into office he did not donate the factories to the workers; he sold them gratis to Western capital! In this way the legitimate democratic aspirations of the peoples of eastern Europe were manipulated and derailed, just as easily as the leftist majorities in the rest of Europe were turned into accomplices of the prevailing imperialist project.

The geometry of possible alliances between the United States, Europe and Russia will weigh heavily on the determination of future globalization. Two configurations are possible here: the first governed by a privileged Euro-Russian partnership, the second by the consolidation of a 'Russian–American alliance' based on Russia's choice to become a major exporter of oil to the United States. The 'common fight against terrorism' since 11 September 2001 has apparently consolidated this alliance. It is clear that we are dealing with a completely asymmetrical partnership, which is nothing other than the implementation of Washington's plan to destroy Russia. Far from providing Russia with the means to modernize its production system, this partnership is closely linked with the interests of the Russian oligarchy and its submission to the project of the transformation of Russia exclusively into a supplier of raw materials. Furthermore, it has facilitated the penetration of the United States into Caucasia and central Asia, from which Moscow is currently being ousted. This configuration cannot therefore constitute an element of the construction of an alternative globalization.

Perhaps the second configuration can. A Euro-Russian partnership could be devised from a different perspective if it did not limit itself to favouring the export of Russian oil to Europe but was accompanied by Europe's active support for the modernization of the whole of the Russian production system. Europe could have taken the initiative at any time since 1990 and proposed a partnership capable of reinforcing the autonomy of the two partners vis-à-vis the United States. Europe, apprehensive as usual, did not do this, afraid of clashing with Washington. It thus opened the way for the US offensive directed at Moscow. Russian oil is therefore destined primarily to meet American needs and is sold in dollars. A partnership that could have planned its sales giving priority to Europe and in euros would have significantly reduced European dependence on suppliers largely controlled by Washington, whether we are talking about the Middle East, the Caspian Sea or the Gulf of Guinea. Europe has therefore accepted this extremely unequal division of the remains of the former Soviet world: Russia and central Asia for the United States; Poland and the Baltic states for the Europeans!

It is not too late to consider reversing Russia's alliances. Opposition to the oligarchy's monopoly of power is gaining ground in Russia. Diplomatic setbacks both in Russia and in Europe in the light of Washington's offensive should provoke reconsideration on all sides. A rapprochement between the large partners of Eurasia (Europe, Russia, China and India) involving the rest of the old world (Africa in particular) is necessary and possible, and would put an end once and for all to Washington's plans to extend the Monroe doctrine to the entire planet. We must head in this direction, with patience certainly, but above all with determination.

CHAPTER 4

India, a great power?

On the way to exceeding even China, with a population of over a billion people and an economic growth rate that is above the world average, India is readily identified as one of the growing powers of the twenty-first century. The purpose of this chapter is to express my doubts regarding this prognosis, as the conditions necessary for India to succeed in becoming a great 'modern' power seem to me to be far from present.

My doubts derive from the crucial importance of the fact that independent India has not tackled the major challenge it faces of radically transforming structures inherited from its colonial capitalist past. Indubitably, the ruling class of independent India decided to graft a 'national bourgeois' plan onto this legacy, which for the most part has been preserved. By examining the successes, limitations and even the failures of this project, I shall pose the question which dominant 'modernized liberalist' discourse has evaded from the outset: whether the bourgeoisie of this country is condemned to subscribe to the compradorization inherent in the status of the peripheral capitalist structures of the country and if, consequently, its accession to the status of great modern power is impossible without undergoing real social revolution (which does not seem to be the order of the day in the foreseeable future).

The colonial inheritance

British colonization essentially transformed India into a dependent agricultural capitalist country. To this end, the British systematically established forms of private ownership of agricultural land that excluded the majority of the peasantry from access to it. This reorganization gave rise to the development of large dominant estates in the north of the country but was less disadvantageous to the medium-sized properties of the comparatively comfortably off peasantry of the south. The majority of the peasants found themselves transformed into a poor, practically landless, peasantry. The price paid for taking this 'capitalist approach' to agricultural development is the incredibly poverty-stricken conditions in which the vast majority of Indian people live.

The widely accepted way of organizing land management is not through private ownership, as modern minds deformed by Eurocentrism automatically believe, but ownership emanating from a political community. In pre-colonial India, it was the village communities that handled access to land (on the basis of highly inegalitarian principles related to the hierarchical caste system). These, in turn, were subject to a superior political community, the state (which levied taxes on the communities under its authority). The British promoted those responsible for this political management, with varying degrees of authority, to the rank of 'private owners'. They thus imposed the particular model of Western capitalism, which has become 'universal', as other Europeans did elsewhere, in America and in the colonies of Asia and Africa. Today, World Bank officials do not have the intellectual means to comprehend that what they recommend as the sole universal approach (private ownership of the land) is merely an exceptional approach whose success in one small part of the world hides the fact that, in general (in other words, for the 'rest of the world'), it is a blind alley.

At the outset, Indian communists recommended that this legacy be challenged and subscribed to the most radical form of their programme of agrarian reform ('land for those who till it'; that is to say, for practically all peasants). The bourgeois in Congress never carried it through, and independent India reduced its promises to the peasantry to a semblance of agrarian reform with no real impact. The fact remains that when the local communist powers went as far as the Indian constitution allowed, as in Western Bengal and Kerala, the positive results recorded in social and economic terms were significant, and popular support for the promoters of the reforms was reinforced.

However, although the fundamental question of the ownership of agricultural land had formerly been one of the major areas of debate within communism and elsewhere among 'progressive' forces (including the democratic bourgeois and populists), the penetration of liberal ideology after the Second World War (even before its apparently total triumph at the end of the century) succeeded in imposing the ('mistaken') idea that the private ownership of land was 'essential', that there was no alternative to the Western approach (disappearance of the peasantry absorbed by urban capitalist development) and that the demand for agrarian reform was therefore 'outdated'. The World Bank put the 'green revolution' and supposed forms of 'market-supported agrarian reforms' in its place. Their implementation always had disastrous results, reinforcing social inequality and increasing the submission of agricultural producers to dominant capital (which was in fact the real, though unacknowledged, objective of these policies). India is a fine example of this. We also know that the market-supported agrarian reforms implemented by the World Bank from Brazil to South Africa became farcical. Unfortunately, the 'revolutionary' left today is largely contaminated by the nonsense propagated by liberal ideology. As for the traditionalists, who aim to re-establish the original 'authentic' social order, they are careful not to challenge this legacy of colonization that benefits the privileged minorities! 'Hindus' here, like the defenders of political Islam elsewhere (Pakistan in particular), submissively subscribe to the expansion of dependent peripheral capitalism.

In India, the hindrance to progress constituted by this colonial inheritance is aggravated by the persistence of the caste system. People of the lowest caste (today known as Dalits) and the tribal populations given the same status account for a quarter of the population of India (around 250 million people). Devoid of all rights, access to land in particular, they are a mass of 'quasi-slaves' and are the collective property of the 'others'. Their low status, which is something akin to that of the Helots of Sparta, allows the others to draw on this mass of available workers for any task and period of time that suits them in return for a mere pittance. The persistence of this situation reinforces the reactionary ideas and behaviour of the 'others' and benefits the exercise of power by and to the benefit of the privileged minority. It plays a part in attenuating and even neutralizing any protest by the exploited majority, who are stuck between the minority exploiters and the oppressed status of the Dalit community.

Of course, British colonization was careful not to challenge the organization in question, hiding behind the hypocritical pretence of 'respecting tradition' (which the British did not do when it did not suit them, for example when privatizing the ownership of land!). Colonial power simultaneously manipulated the situation to its own benefit by allowing some Dalit access through education to collaborative positions. It could be said that governments in independent India have continued this tradition, which was only seriously questioned during the short time the left alliance led by V.P. Singh (supported by the communists) was in power. The Hindu right has, of course, nothing to say on the subject. And the United States today – through the intermediary of NGOs 'defending human rights' – tries to manipulate the Dalit community's protests in the same way and to contain them in inoffensive spaces for the management of capitalism as a whole.

Fortunately, this situation may be in the process of being overcome by the radicalization of the struggle in the form of uprisings, led by 'Naxalite' Maoist peasants in particular. It is true that these uprisings have been put down, in the sense that they have not managed to establish and stabilize popular power in liberated regions, but they have, nonetheless, taken steps to challenge the property structures inherited from colonialism and the caste system, and in doing so may have paved the way for revolutionary mobilizations to come. The arrival of the Dalit on the political scene, a major social event in the last two decades, is, without doubt, in part the product of Naxalism.

Success and limitations of the populist national project

The Congress governments of independent India implemented a national plan typical of its time influenced by the victories of the national liberation movements of Asia and Africa after the Second World War. The parties (political forces that were mobilized during this struggle for independence, modernization and development) henceforth in power enjoyed undeniable legitimacy but the plans they put into effect were undermined by the ambiguities that characterized the liberation movements themselves. These plans were anti-imperialist inasmuch as they fully understood that modernization and development required national liberation first of all, but they stopped there, believing they could impose the necessary adjustments on the globally dominant system (world capitalism), allowing the nations of Asia and Africa to establish themselves as equal partners and by this means progressively overcome the handicaps of their 'backwardness'. In spite of their successes, never negligible, they did not achieve this and rapidly encountered the limitations of their strategic ideas.

The debates of the time – in India as elsewhere in Asia and Africa – specifically concerned these strategic ideas. Was it a necessary stage, described in the Marxist jargon of the time as a 'revolutionary democratic bourgeois' phase, which was preparing for its own move to the left by shifting to 'the construction of socialism'?

Beyond its established national dimension, the plan of those in power included 'social constituents' of greater or lesser significance, which the broad alliance of the people against imperialism probably imposed even on those in the dominant classes who could see no further than the benefits of capitalism. Across the various situations, one common denominator connected all the legitimate powers that originated from national liberation: namely, their 'populist' character – that is, on the one hand, their will to ensure the benefits of development were shared by the whole (or the majority) of society, and, on the other, their desire to control the process by depriving the dominated classes of the opportunity to organize themselves freely beyond their control.

The communists have often expressed a clear awareness of this contradiction and the limitations that it imposed on the system's achievements, but (for various reasons that I will not enter into here as I have done so elsewhere), like others under the influence of the Soviets (and attitudes recommended by them, argued in terms of the 'non-capitalist approach'), the majority of communists in Asia and in Africa ended up becoming (to a greater or lesser extent 'critical') forces of support for the populist national plans in question. The split that pitted Maoism against the Soviets sometimes curbed the extent of this support in Asia in particular. On the whole, in this respect, the Indian communists (both the Communist Party–Marxist-Leninist, and the Communist Party–Marxist) kept their distance from Congress's populist national plan, the exception being the Communist Party of India (CPI), which for this reason is today marginalized. The Indian communists, therefore, held a strong position within their society that cannot be compared, for example, with that of the Arab communists, whose parties almost unconditionally rallied to Nasserist, Baathist and Boumédienne-style populism.

In spite of their limitations, the successes of Nehru and Indira Gandhi's Indian populist national plan were significant both in economic and in political terms. From the outset, colonization carried out a systematic deindustrialization of India – which had been advanced at the time – to the benefit of Great Britain, which was in the process of industrialization, so independent India gave priority to its reindustrialization. This was envisioned with a high degree of systematization, at least in the period of the early plans during the time of Nehru, and combined large private Indian industrial capital with public-sector enterprises promoted to fill the shortcomings in the production system inherited from colonization, to accelerate growth and reinforce basic industries.

The macropolitics of regulation implemented at that time were designed to serve this modernization plan. Price and foreign exchange control, subsidies, regulation of foreign enterprises, borrowed technology were used to secure the main objective of protecting Indian industry from the devastating effects of domination of the world markets by imperialist capital. Only secondarily did the regulations in question pursue social objectives – the redistribution of wealth, but above all a reduction of the extreme poverty of the popular classes. This accelerated industrial modernization plan, accompanied by a plan to develop agricultural production (food crops in particular) based on what has been called the 'green' revolution (which replaced the abandoned agrarian reform – the 'red revolution'!), was destined principally to make the country self-sufficient in terms of food in order to allow it to channel all its export revenue exclusively to covering the imports needed by its industry.

The whole plan was well and truly capitalist in nature in the sense that the benefits of production and the technologies chosen did not challenge the fundamental rationale of capitalism, although it could be said, in this respect, that the experience of actually existing socialism (even in China) was not very different in spite of the exclusively public property in this case. The Indian plan was, however, less radical in the sense that the degree of its production system's disconnection from the dominant world system was less systematic than it was in the USSR or China, where wages and prices – in theory planned – were really detached from any comparison with those of the global capitalist system. This characteristic of the Indian plan, which can be found in other non-communist populist national experiences (in the Arab world, for example), was closely linked to the failure to challenge social structures inherited from colonization.

The full extent of this close relationship was revealed through the option of the 'green revolution', which we know reinforced rather than weakened the position of the dominant rural classes and large property owners in particular.

These differences between the national Indian model and that of Communist China account for the visible differences in the results they brought about. The growth rate of industrial and agricultural production in India was not 'bad' at that time; it was significantly higher than it had been during colonial times and above the world average for post-war capitalism, even though it was booming, but on the whole it remained at a considerably lower level than that of China. Moreover, whereas growth in China was accompanied by a marked improvement in the popular classes' standard of living, this was not the case in India, where growth exclusively benefited the new middle classes (who were the minority although their expansion accelerated to the point of increasing in a period of some thirty years from 5 to 15 per cent of the overall population of the country); the poverty of the dominant popular classes remained unchanged, even worsened slightly.

Liberal discourse does not take these basic realities into account, which is why I do not subscribe to the 'optimistic' conclusions drawn by many 'futurologists', according to which India is in the process of pursuing accelerated growth which will raise it to the status of a great modern power, following China's example. Until now, China has had the advantage of the legacy of its radical revolution, whereas India is handicapped by the unchallenged legacy of colonization. This is why economic growth in China, supported by investment systems that are more favourable to the development of the whole production system, continues to exceed that of India and is accompanied by a pattern of redistribution of income more favourable (or less unfavourable) to the popular classes. The fact remains that if China were to become too 'liberal' and India were to pursue the ultraliberal option as it has done over the last fifteen years or so, we would not see the growth rate accelerate; on the contrary, it would flag, placing China alongside India, even resulting in reductions in the rates in both countries. In my opinion, the 'agrarian question' lies at the heart of the challenge the two countries are currently facing, by which I mean the fundamental question of the access of all the peasantry to land and production, access that people still have today in China (for how long?) but that is always denied in India.

For their part, the political successes of independent India are certainly significant. Unlike China, India is a multinational country. It was only by playing precisely on the diversity of its Indian peoples (and states) that British colonization succeeded in imposing its power. Credit is due to the national liberation movement for its success in this domain, which is unrivalled in the colonial world. This movement really succeeded in uniting the ten great nations of which the country is made up into one single 'nation'. It matters little that the name of this nation ('Bharat', giving rise to the concept of Bharatva, which can be translated as 'Indianness') seems 'debatable' from a 'scientific' (or para-scientific) point of view. Since then, India has well and truly been one nation, the reality of which is obvious to all of its constituent parts, and to this day this common sense of belonging prevails over specific local factors (linguistic among others). The national liberation movement had only one failing in this respect, which lay in its desire to involve the Muslims in the creation of the new Indian nation. Here, the British succeeded in undermining the Indian national plan and forcing through the creation of the artificial states of Pakistan and Bangladesh. The fact remains that even if the Muslims who remained in India (approximately 15 per cent of the total population) sometimes seemed to 'pose a problem' (a problem that Hindu culturalists unjustifiably exploit), they are fully and properly integrated into all aspects of the social and political life of the country. The reason for this success is the secularism of the Indian state, which even the wave of Hindu culturalism has not succeeded in undermining. The difference in the behaviour of Indian governments and the majority of Indian society towards its Muslim 'minority' and the behaviour of Muslim-dominated governments and societies towards their Christian minorities, for example, demonstrates the value of secularism.

This democratic progress is not found in other regions of the world (the Arab and Muslim world in particular).

Of course, this assertion needs to be qualified. The repression of the Sikhs' demands (which cost the life of Indira Gandhi) and the situation in Kashmir are evidence of the limitations of the regime's capacity to deal with 'national questions' (even if they are described in other terms). Yet the fact remains that the powers in Delhi have found ways to handle problems successfully with all the great peoples of the 'Indo-Aryan' north and the 'Dravidian' south, and thus make federal unity – which is in fact far more centralized than the terms of the constitution provide for – a solid reality.

The experience of modern-day India demonstrates the unquestionable superiority of democracy and the futility of arguments in support of an autocratic management that claims to be more effective. This remains true despite the evident limitations and the class content of bourgeois democracy in general, and the reality of it in India's experience. To the credit of the national liberation movement (Congress and the communists), this option was probably the only effective way of managing the various social and regional interests (even if limited to those of the privileged classes) and winning popular support for the plan of the minority making up the hegemonic bloc.

On the international scene, independent India applied itself to shaping the 'southern front' of the time, the Non-Aligned Movement, whose origins lay in the Afro-Asian Conference held in Bandung (1955); not even its head-on collision with China called this overtly anti-imperialist strategy into question.

The liberal and culturalist drift

The erosion of the national populist plan was as unavoidable in India as it was elsewhere on account of its inherent limitations and contradictions. This and the delegitimization of power that accompanied it gave rise to an offensive by obscurantist forces which was supported by the dominant comprador class and a large proportion of the middle classes (whose expansion was decelerating and increasingly beset by difficulties) who were motivated by the discourse (and manoeuvres) of US imperialism.

In India, these obscurantist illusions have a name: Hindutva. This term designates the affirmation of the priority of adherence to the Hindu religion defined as the 'real identity' of the peoples of the country, as opposed to the concept of 'Bharatva', which refers to the nation. Of course, this 'Hindu' affirmation does not challenge the colonial legacy concerning land ownership or respect for the hierarchical caste system in particular. In this regard, as Indian communists have not ceased to point out, the obscurantist illusions serve the interests of comprador and imperialist powers perfectly. The 'specificities' with which their para-'national', even para-anti-imperialist, discourse is filled are absolutely worthless. They fuel a renewal of the practice of the (in this case anti-Muslim) 'communitarism' that colonial power used, in its day, to counter the rising aspirations of secular, democratic, modernist national liberation.

Nothing in this respect differentiates this regression from that which afflicts other peripheral societies that are victims of the same erosion of the national populist plan, Arab and Muslim societies in particular. The parallel with political Islam can be observed here.

Nevertheless, this adverse drift does not necessarily seem to be as marked in India as in Arab and Muslim countries. The reason for this no doubt lies in the fact that Indian communist parties kept their distance from the Congress's plan for independent India, whereas those of Arab and Muslim countries rallied almost unconditionally to similar populist plans. As a result of this, the communists in India maintained a certain degree of (even growing) popularity, which protected society from regression, at the very time when almost everywhere else in the world they were entering a phase of decline (electoral in particular).

The decline was therefore accompanied here by the renewed radicalization of social struggles. Evidence of this can be seen in the Naxalite offensive, which, in spite of their error of judgement regarding the real balance of forces in Indian society, did reawaken revolutionary awareness among the peasantry in vast areas (approximately a third) of India. Further evidence can be seen in the brutal entry of the Dalit into political and social struggle (no doubt a result of the radicalization of the peasantry), and in the confirmed attachment of all of the middle classes to democracy, even to secularism. The communist parties themselves, and the Communist Party–Marxist in particular, were not unaffected by this radicalization.

This explains why the collapse of the legitimacy which Congress had enjoyed almost exclusively did not produce a 'definitive victory' (even provisional) for the right. A first right-wing government was overturned by a left-wing electoral alliance led by V.P. Singh, who offered the communists greater influence in the political life of the country. This still fragile alliance was unable to prevent the electoral recovery of the right but, in turn, this second experience of a 'Hindu-comprador' government, which wholly subscribed to the dictates of imperialism on the offensive (accelerating economic 'liberalization'), well and truly failed. The last elections (2004) put paid to the right's plan and, through the rejection of this plan by the majority of the Indian electorate, the premises of 'Hindu culturalism' and liberalism promoted by the comprador bourgeoisie and its imperialist masters were jointly held responsible for the social catastrophe. This association is not made elsewhere, in the Arab and Muslim worlds in particular.

This being the case, the battle is far from being won by the Indian left. The effects of the erosion of the forms of political management associated with the populist national phase (itself produced by the former national liberation movement) that are found elsewhere characterize India today. By this I mean the loss of credibility of undemocratic forms of organization and forms of fighting 'commanded from on high by ruling cliques' to which the communist parties themselves are not strangers. The conflict between the (supposedly spontaneous) 'movement of the popular classes' and the 'aspiration for participatory democracy/parties and formal organizations' is as typical of India as it is of the whole of the modern world. The formation of an alternative, which will be difficult, must meet this challenge.

The long and difficult march of alternative globalization

Dominant liberal discourse not only considers there to be 'no alternative' to 'economic liberalism' and the accompanying form of globalization, but also deems that support for this choice is progressive and that everyone endowed with an entrepreneurial spirit can only be a 'winner'. It is not enough to recognize that is factually nonsense and does not stand up to serious theoretical reflection. Building a progressive social alternative that would form part of a real alter-globalization is still difficult and the march in this direction long.

Where India is concerned, the creation of such an alternative necessarily means that appropriate, progressive responses must be found to meet the four main challenges.

First challenge: to find a radical solution to the Indian peasant problem based on the recognition of the right of all peasants to access to land in the most egalitarian conditions possible. This, in turn, means the abolition of the caste system and the ideology that legitimizes it. In other words, India must engage in as radical a revolution as that of China, or at least undertake far-reaching reforms that would ensure significant progress in this direction. The current peasant struggles are certainly not negligible: their frequency, the geographical area they cover and the violence that accompanies them speak for themselves. However, they remain confused and pursue different and at times contradictory objectives. The best organized struggles – those that are occasionally victorious here and there, or at least succeed in forcing the authorities to pull back – are those of the modern-day peasantry whose demands are in line with capitalist and market thinking, and make demands relating to the management of prices, and conditions for access to inputs and to credit. This explains why these struggles are often led by rich members of the peasantry, themselves also victims of the current phase of demands imposed by global capitalism, the comprador class and the state at its service. The struggles of the poor and landless, including the Dalit, are for the most part private explosions of long-term strategic visions. Clearly, it falls to the communists in this respect not only to revive their 'reflection' but also to contribute to the creation of suitable forms of peasant organization, which is clearly necessary if effective strategies are to materialize.

Second challenge: to create a united workers' front that integrates segments of the relatively stabilized working classes and those that are not. This challenge is common to all countries of the modern world and particularly all those of the periphery of the system that are characterized by the enormously destructive effects of the new poverty (massive unemployment, lack of job security, excrescence of wretched 'informal' conditions). It must be recognized that the working-class organizations which the national liberation movement, including the communists, succeeded in 'mobilizing' with some degree of effectiveness, thus forming the social basis of the political forces of the former 'left', are today faced with a challenge of unprecedented proportions. The social commitments of the past, between capital, the state and factions of the working classes (unionists in particular) are challenged by the imperialist and comprador offensive, while new social structures have meant that earlier forms of organization and action have lost their effectiveness. It is the duty of the unionists, communists and activists of popular movements to open the debate on these questions and invent new forms that will advance participatory democracy and together be capable of defining the stages of a common long-term strategy.

Third challenge: to maintain the unity of the Indian subcontinent, and to renew the forms of association of the various peoples that make up the Indian nation on strengthened democratic foundations. To defeat the strategies of imperialism, which, as always, pursues, beyond its tactical options, its objective of disempowering the 'great states', which are better able than micro-states to withstand the assaults of imperialism.

Fourth challenge: to focus international political options on the central issue of reconstructing a 'front of the peoples of the South' (the solidarity of the peoples of Asia and Africa first and foremost) in circumstances that, of course, are no longer those that presided over the formation of the Non-Aligned Movement at the 'time of Bandung' (1955–75). To give the highest priority to the objective of derailing the United States plan for military control of the planet and thwarting the political manoeuvres of Washington, whose purpose is to prevent any serious rapprochement between India, China and Russia.

The political and social forces that prevent India from moving in the above-mentioned directions are considerable. They constitute a 'hegemonic bloc' that accounts for a fifth of the population – behind the great industrial, commercial and financial bourgeoisie and the big landowners, the great mass of well-off peasants and middle classes, the high bureaucracy and technocracy. These 200 million Indians are the exclusive beneficiaries of the national plan implemented so far. No doubt, at the present time of extreme liberal triumph, this bloc is collapsing under the effect, among others, of the end of the upward social mobility of the lower middle classes who are threatened with loss of job security, even impoverishment, if not outright poverty. This situation provides the left with the opportunity to develop tactics, if it can, to weaken the coherence of these reactionary forces in general and in particular their comprador approach, which is the driving force of globalized imperialist domination. However, it also offers opportunities to the Hindu right if the left fails.

It is often said in India that this 'nation of 200 million people' – which alone constitutes a large market comparable to that of several large European countries – was the country's future, whereas the majority, who number some 800 million poverty-stricken Indians, are nothing but a ball and chain shackled to it. Besides being abhorrent (should the poor be exterminated?), this reactionary opinion is utterly stupid. The 'minority' is only privileged because it exploits the country's resources and workers, who are the majority.

The minority that make up this bloc are, therefore, in a situation that excludes the reproduction in India of the historic capital–labour compromise on which the social democracy of the developed West was founded. And the discourse that compares 'peripheral Fordism' to the Fordism that is characteristic of developed regions is based on a huge failure to understand the impact of each of these two formulas: Western Fordism shared benefits of capitalist expansion with the majority of the working classes; peripheral Fordism operates for the sole benefit of the 'middle classes'. India is not the only example of this: Brazil and China today are in similar situations.

The management of the coherence of this hegemonic bloc through political democracy, such as in India, does not lessen its reactionary class dimension. On the contrary, it is the most effective way to establish it. This hegemonic bloc is well and truly 'integrated' into the rationale of dominant capitalist globalization, and so far none of the various political forces through which it is expressed challenges it. It is therefore clear why the 'Indian national project' remains fragile, vulnerable and incapable of delivering its own stated objective, which is to transform India into 'a large modern capitalist power'.

This vulnerability results in the frequently opportunistic behaviour of the Indian political class, justified most often by short-term 'realpolitik' arguments. Faced with the United States plan for 'overall (military) control of the planet' and the collective imperialist alignment of the triad (United States, Europe and Japan), in spite of the concerns of some of its partners, the Indian political class has so far been incapable of producing and implementing the necessary countermeasures. That would entail the creation of a front uniting India, Russia and China, all threatened in equal measure by the compradorization resulting from the expansion of the new collective imperialism. It might also entail the more systematic pursuit of a rapprochement with Europe, depending on the extent to which the latter keeps its distance from Washington's leading plan. India's rulers do not think this likely, including those associated with the most committed government formulas to undermine the Hindu/comprador right. On the contrary, they continue to give priority to their 'conflicts' with China, perceived as a potential military adversary and a dangerous financial rival on the markets of globalized capitalism. They even believe they may be able to 'use' a possible rapprochement with the United States in order to become its major ally in Asia. There are others in the third world that have similar reasoning: Brazil, South Africa and even China.

The measures necessary to counter the deployment of the new collective imperialism require the reconstruction of a southern peoples' front. Here again, the task is far from easy. The conflicts between the countries of the South, especially in the area between India and Pakistan, largely caused by 'culturalist/comprador' deviation (for which the responsibility of political Islam is considerable), take precedence and reinforce the short-term tactical calculations of the Indian political class.

This opportunism will not only in the long term destroy the conditions necessary for construction of both a progressive national alternative and an alter-globalization to support it; it blinds its defenders to the point of making them lose sight of the vulnerability of Indian unity and any manoeuvres by imperialism, which seeks to destroy it. There should be no illusions on this score. Even if today Washington diplomacy chooses to 'support India and its unity' for a while and for tactical reasons, its long-term plan is to disable the capacity of this great country to become a great power. Submitting to demands to subscribe to the expansion of global capitalism reinforces centrifugal tendencies, for this submission accentuates the 'regional' inequalities of development. Do we not already hear the 'privileged classes' of Bangalore (who have benefited from the expansion of new technologies) say that an independent Karnataka would profit more from current globalization than the Indian state of Karnataka?

CHAPTER 5

Can solidarity be rebuilt
among the countries of the South?

The United Nations named the 1960s and 1970s 'development decades'. That is indeed what they were, if we judge them not only in terms of economic growth rates (nearly everywhere incomparably higher than in the colonial era or, in most cases, than in the new age of liberal globalization that would follow) but also by the social upheavals and gigantic policies that gave the three continents a shape quite unlike that of former times.

The 1960s and 1970s were also marked by strong solidarity among the states of Asia and post-colonial Africa. This showed itself not only in their economic demands – which forced the international institutions, including the World Bank and the IMF, to sit up and take notice – but also in their political support for the struggles of colonial peoples, their refusal to join military alliances that complemented Nato, and so on. In a sense, then, we may describe it as a period of multipolarity, however uneven. The countries of the South 'counted' in the international order; the globalization of the time was at least partly 'negotiated'.

Evidently that solidarity no longer exists. Why is this so? Should it be reconstituted? On what basis? To answer these questions, we first need to draw up a critical balance sheet of the period in question (the 'Bandung era' from 1955 to 1975), then to identify the new challenges, to formulate the aims of a solidarity that might give rise to a new multipolarity, and to consider the conditions under which progress in that direction might be made.

A critical balance sheet of the 'Bandung era', 1955–75

In 1955 the main heads of state in the newly independent countries of Asia and Africa met for the first time in Bandung. The regimes they headed still had very little experience, and the struggle to complete the historical task of independence was not yet over. The first Vietnam war had scarcely finished and the second was already looming on the horizon; the Korean War had ended in the status quo ante; the Algerian war was in full swing; the decolonization of sub-Saharan Africa was not yet on the agenda; and the Palestinian drama was still in its early stages.

The Asian and African leaders who gathered in Bandung were far from identical to one another. The political and ideological currents they represented, their visions of the society they wished to construct or reconstruct, and their relations with the West were all areas of difference. Nevertheless, a common project brought them closer together and gave sense to their meeting. The common minimum programme included completion of the political decolonization of Asia and Africa, but they were also agreed that political independence was only an instrument: the final aim was economic, social and cultural liberation. Then, however, two rival visions divided the participants: a majority thought that development was possible in a framework of 'interdependence' within the world economy, while the Communist minority thought that a break with the capitalist camp would lead to the construction of a world socialist camp – with, if not behind, the USSR.

The leaders of the capitalist third world, who did not think in terms of 'delinking' or leaving the system, did not agree among themselves on a single strategic and tactical vision of development. In varying degrees, however, they thought that the building of a developed, independent economy and society (albeit in a context of global interdependence) entailed some degree of conflict with the dominant West; and a more radical wing considered it necessary to end the control over their national economies by the capital of foreign monopolies.

Eager to preserve their newly won independence, these leaders refused to join the global military game by providing bases for the encirclement of the socialist countries that US hegemonism sought to impose. But they also insisted that this did not mean they had to place themselves under the protection of America's adversary, the Soviet Union. Hence the 'neutralism' or 'non-alignment' that came to identify the group of countries, and the ongoing organization, that emerged from the spirit of Bandung.

The links among African and Asian states had already been fore-shadowed by an Arab–Asian group within the United Nations. Bandung then strengthened this tendency and gave considerable fresh momentum to the anti-colonial struggle. Three years later, in liberated Accra, Kwame Nkrumah declared that 'Africa must unite'. But, after the collapse of Nkrumah's pan-Africanism and the powerlessness of the Casablanca Group and the Monrovia Group to deliver any results in the Congo, between 1960 and 1963, Africa united only in the minimal form of con-stituting the Organization of African Unity (OAU), in 1963.

As summit meetings succeeded one another in the 1960s and 1970s, the institutionalized 'Non-Aligned Movement' embracing nearly all the countries of Asia and Africa gradually shifted away from a front of political solidarity with liberation struggles and a rejection of military pacts, to become a kind of 'trade union fighting for economic demands vis-à-vis the North'. In this framework, the Non-Aligned Movement eventually allied itself with the Latin American countries (except Cuba), which had never dreamed of opposing the hegemonism of the United States. The Group of 77 (the whole of the third world) gave expression to this new broad alliance of the South. The struggle for a 'new inter-national economic order', launched in 1975 after the October War of 1973 and the oil price hikes, crowned this whole tendency but also sounded its death knell.

Neither politically nor economically did the Bandung spirit fill the hearts of the West with joy. Indeed, the hatred that the Western powers reserved for radical third world leaders of the 1960s (Nasser, Sukarno, Nkrumah, Modibo Keita) – nearly all overthrown in the period from 1965 to 1968, which also saw the Israeli attack of June 1967 against Egypt, Syria and Jordan – demonstrates that the political vision of non-alignment was never accepted by the powers of the Atlantic Alliance. The non-aligned camp was therefore politically much weakened when it came to face the world economic crisis that broke in 1970–71.

What we may today call 'development ideology', now in a state of crisis that may prove terminal, passed through its heyday in these years between 1955 and 1975. The political economy of non-alignment, though often vague and merely implicit, may be defined in terms of the following components:

- a will to develop the productive forces and to diversify production, especially through industrialization;
- a determination that the national state should have leadership and control of the process;
- a belief that technical models are 'neutral', though requiring control, and that there is no alternative but to reproduce them;
- a belief that the development process mainly requires not popular initiative but only popular support for state action;
- a belief that the process does not fundamentally clash with trade participation in the world capitalist system, even if it brings temporary conflicts with it.

Up to a certain point, the circumstances of capitalist expansion in the years between 1955 and 1970 made it easier for this project to score some successes. After four decades of post-war development, the balance sheet is so patchy that one is tempted to give up the term 'third world' as a single referent for the countries that were the object of development policies during that time. The tendency today, not without reason, is to contrast a newly industrialized and partly competitive third world (the so-called 'emergent economies') with a marginal 'fourth world' of countries excluded from the process.

Despite differences in the accompanying ideological discourse, the aim of development policies in Asia, Africa and Latin America was essentially the same: to speed up the modernization and enrichment of the national society by means of its industrialization. This common denominator will be easy to grasp if we recall that in 1945 virtually all the countries of Asia (except Japan), Africa (including South Africa) and, with a few minor qualifications, Latin America still lacked any industry worthy of the name, apart from a few mining installations here and there; their population was largely rural, and they were either placed under colonial rule (Africa, India, Southeast Asia) or governed by archaic regimes such as the latifundista oligarchies of Latin America or the monarchical protectorates of the Islamic East and China. Over and above their great diversity, therefore, all the national liberation movements set themselves the goals of political independence, state modernization and economic industrialization.

It would be wrong to say that they did not all try to attain these goals, once they were in a position to do so. To be sure, there were almost as many variants as there were countries, and so it is analytically legitimate to classify them into a number of models. But then one risks becoming the victim of the selection criteria – not necessarily of one's ideological preferences, but at least of one's own idea (or the idea that people had at the time) of the experiments in question and the external or internal possibilities and constraints under which they operated. On the other hand, in emphasizing the common denominator that united them, I am suggesting that we take a certain distance from the classificatory schemas and interpret history from the vantage point of today – in other words, that we reread the history in the light of what it actually led to.

To industrialize meant first of all to build an internal market and to protect it from the otherwise fatal ravages of competition. The formulas varied according to circumstances – size of the internal market, availability of resources – or even according to the theoretical/ideological emphasis on one of two priorities: either the rapid development of light industry to produce consumption goods here and now, or an initial boosting of heavy industry to produce the conditions for a more rapid production of consumption goods later on (a rationalization of the traditional Soviet positions). But the final goal in either case was the same. The technology necessary for industrialization had to be imported, but this did not mean it was not necessary to accept that foreign capital should own the industrial plant. It all depended on the bargaining power of the country in question. Similarly, the capital to fund industrial development could be either borrowed or attracted to invest in the country. Or, once again, the precise formula – foreign private ownership, public funding through a combination of national savings and external aid in the form of gifts or loans – could be adjusted to an estimate of the likely costs and benefits. The import needs inherent in plans to speed up growth through industrialization could, in the early stages, be covered only through the familiar traditional exports, whether agricultural products or minerals. That was certainly a possibility. In a period of general growth, such as that which followed the Second World War, demand was constantly rising for all manner of products (energy, raw materials, particular agricultural goods). The terms of trade fluctuated, but any deterioration did not systematically wipe out the effects of the growing volume of exports.

Modernization, though geared to industrialization, was not reducible to it. Urbanization, the development of transport and communications, education and social services, certainly had the partial aim of supplying new industries with infrastructure and skilled manpower. But we can tell from the (almost intrinsically transethnic) nationalist discourse of the time that they also served as ends in themselves, as part of the construction of a modern state and the general modernization of behaviour.

Of course, unlike today, the talk then was not constantly of an opposition between 'state intervention' and 'private interests' – the one supposedly running counter to, and the other favouring, spontaneous market tendencies. In fact, the common wisdom among governments at the time saw state intervention as a key element in the construction of the market and modernization. The radical left, socialist-leaning in its reading of ideology, certainly associated the spread of statism with the gradual elimination of private property. But the nationalist right, which did not share that objective, was no less statist and interventionist: it rightly believed that the construction of private interests demanded vigorous intervention by the state. In those days, the nonsense that is now the stuff of ruling discourses would have failed to elicit any response.

There is now a strong temptation to read this as a phase in the expansion of world capitalism – a phase which, with varying degrees of success, accomplished certain functions of national primitive accumulation and thereby paved the way for the present opening to the world market and global competition. I shall not give in to the temptation, however. The dominant forces in world capitalism did not 'spontaneously' create the model or models of development; they had 'development' imposed on them. It was the product of the third world national liberation movement of the time. My own reading of the history would therefore emphasize the contradiction between the spontaneous, immediate tendencies of the capitalist system, always guided by short-term financial calculation, and the longer-term visions that drive rising political forces in conflict with those immediate tendencies. To be sure, it is not always a deep-seated conflict; capitalism can adjust to it, not being the underlying cause of its motion.

In this framework, the conflict between the dominant forces of world capitalism and the driving forces of the Bandung 'developmentalist' project was more or less radical according to whether statism was meant to supplant capitalism or to sustain it. The radical wing of the movement did clash with the immediate interests of dominant capitalism, especially as a result of its nationalizations and its refusal to accept foreign ownership. The moderate wing agreed to look for middle ground between the conflicting interests and therefore offered greater opportunities for capital to adjust. At an international level, this distinction closely followed the terms of the East–West conflict between Sovietism and Western capitalism.

All the national liberation movements shared this modernist (hence capitalist and bourgeois) vision. That is not to say they were inspired, still less directed, by a bourgeoisie in the full sense of the term, which barely existed at the time of independence and, even thirty years later, remained at best no more than embryonic. But the ideology of modernization did exist: it was the main force giving meaning to the popular revolt against colonization. This ideology was the bearer of a project that I would call – perhaps curiously at first sight – 'capitalism without capitalists'. It was *capitalism*, since modernization was conceived as reproducing the essential capitalist relations of production and social relations: the wage relation, company management, urbanization, hierarchical education, a certain type of national citizenship. (Of course, other values characteristic of advanced capitalism, such as political democracy, were cruelly lacking – the usual justification being the demands of the preliminary stage of development; all the countries in question, whether radical or moderate, opted for the same formula of a single party, farcical elections, one great leader–founder of the Fatherland, and so on.) It was *without capitalists* in so far as the state, and its technocrats, were called upon to substitute for a bourgeoisie of entrepreneurs, but also in so far as the emergence of the bourgeoisie was treated with suspicion, because of the priority it would give to its immediate interests over those of long-term economic construction. In the radical wing of the national liberation movement, this suspicion became synonymous with exclusion and the favoured project became one of the 'construction of socialism', in line with Soviet-style discourse. With the aim of 'catching up the West' as its chief preoccupation, this project succeeded through its own dynamic in constructing a 'capitalism without capitalists'.

The national liberation movements divided between 'socialistic' tendencies to radicalism and tendencies to moderation. The opposition based itself on a complex set of causes, sometimes remaining attached to the social classes on which the movement rested (peasantry, popular urban layers, middle classes, privileged classes), sometimes clinging to the traditions in which it had been trained politically and organizationally (metropolitan Communist parties, labour unions, churches).

If we use the criterion of the national liberation movement itself – that is, 'national construction' – the results are generally questionable. For, whereas the development of capitalism in earlier times had bolstered national integration, the globalization operating in the peripheries of the system tended to tear societies apart. The ideology of the national movements made no allowance for this contradiction, remaining trapped in the bourgeois concept of 'closing the historical gap' through participation in the international division of labour (not through its negation: delinking). No doubt the particular features of the pre-colonial, pre-capitalist society made this disintegration effect more or less dramatic. In Africa, where artificial colonial divisions did not respect the previous history of its peoples, the disintegration bound up with its conversion into a periphery of capitalism made it possible for ethnicism to survive, in spite of the efforts of the new national ruling classes to overcome its manifestations. When the crisis struck, suddenly wiping out the surpluses that had funded the transethnic policies of the new state, the ruling class itself broke up into a number of fragments – fragments which, stripped of any legitimacy from the achievements of 'development', often tried to create a new base for themselves by falling back on ethnicism.

If we use the criterion of socialism, the results are even more uneven. Of course, we should understand here by 'socialism' what radical populist ideology made it out to be: a progressive vision emphasizing social mobility, greater equality of incomes, a kind of full employment in urban areas, and a poorer version of the welfare state. In these terms, the achievements of a country like Tanzania present a striking contrast with Zaire, Ivory Coast or Kenya, where inequalities have grown ever sharper over the past forty years, during periods of high economic growth as well as in later periods of stagnation.

Yet the criterion really in keeping with the logic of capitalist expansion is competitiveness on world markets. From this point of view, the results are uneven in the extreme: the group of the main Asian and Latin American countries, which have become competitive industrial exporters, sharply contrast with the whole group of African countries, which remain confined to the export of primary products. The former are the new third world (tomorrow's periphery, in my analysis), while the latter are what are now known as the 'fourth world', doomed to a marginal position in the new stage of capitalist globalization.

The roots of Africa's exclusion

An explanation for Africa's failure must take into account all the complex interactions between its particular internal conditions and the logic of global capitalist expansion. As these interactions are often ignored, the current explanations – those of 'experts in international economics' as well as third world nationalists – do not penetrate beneath the surface.

The international experts stress certain phenomena in isolation from the overall logic of the system – for example, corruption of the political class, fragility of the economic foundations, low agricultural productivity or ethnic fragmentation – and inevitably end up recommending greater insertion into the world capitalist economy. In their view, Africa mainly needs 'real' capitalist entrepreneurs and a shake-up that will break the grip of rural self-sufficiency by systematically promoting commercial agriculture. Such blinkered reasoning abstracts from the wider setting, and ignores the fact that the capitalist road in agriculture would produce a gigantic surplus population which, at the present level of technology, could not be employed in industry as its counterparts were in nineteenth-century Europe. History does not repeat itself.

Third world nationalists emphasize other, no less real phenomena, such as the declining prices of raw materials on which the funding of take-off depends. They also rightly point to the numerous political, and sometimes military, interventions by Western powers hostile to the forces of progressive social change and supportive of reactionary, archaic forces. Their arguments do not, however, structurally engage with the logic of internal conflict, and so they end up counterposing a 'nation' stripped of contradictions to 'the outside world'.

The above analysis of Africa's failure keeps in mind the responsibilities of colonization and the project of ruling classes linked to neocolonialism, just as it builds in aspects of the global geostrategy of imperialism. Once the colonies were conquered, it was obviously necessary to 'valorize' them – to subject them to economic exploitation – and it was here that the logics of world capitalism and the prior history of African societies came into play. We can see the basis for the three models of colonization: (i) incorporation of small farmers into the world 'trade' in tropical products, together with their subjection to controlled monopoly markets that made it possible to keep the payment for agricultural labour to a minimum, at the price of land wastage and other deformations; (ii) the mining-based reservation economy of southern Africa, which drew on cheap forced labour from 'reservations' inadequate to sustain traditional rural self-subsistence; and (iii) the pillage economy through which concession-ary companies raked off a share of the crop without paying anything in return, where local social conditions did not permit 'trading' and the level of mineral wealth did not justify organizing 'reservations' to supply large quantities of cheap labour.

Such modes of insertion into world capitalism eventually proved cata-strophic for the peoples of Africa. Colonization delayed any attempt at agrarian revolution by a century. It was possible to extract a surplus from peasant labour and the wealth of nature, without making any investment in modernization (machinery or fertilizers), without really paying for labour (which was reproduced in the framework of traditional self-sufficiency), and even without maintaining the natural conditions for the reproduction of wealth (through the pillage of agricultural land and forests). At the same time, this mode of exploiting natural wealth, within the framework of the uneven global division of labour of the time, ruled out the formation of a local bourgeoisie. Indeed, whenever the first signs of one appeared, the colonial authorities hastened to put a stop to it.

The weaknesses of the national liberation movement and the post-colonial states can be traced back to these colonial roots. Contrary to the ideology of globalist capitalism, which seeks to legitimize itself through the usual racist discourse, they are not the product of a pre-colonial Africa that disappeared in the upheavals. The 'critics' of independent Africa, who point to its corrupt political bourgeoisies, its lack of economic sense and its communal structures lingering in the countryside, forget that these characteristics of contemporary Africa were forged in the period between 1880 and 1960.

It is therefore not surprising that neocolonialism has perpetuated these characteristics. The political teams responsible for independent Africa, including those who accepted the neocolonial option, were not all artificially constituted out of former colonial agents; their weaknesses were those of peripheral capitalism, as it took shape in these parts. All the same, the metropolises of the North bear a major responsibility for what has happened. Despite the weaknesses of colonial society, the liberation movements produced elites potentially capable of going further than they did; the fact is that every effort was made to scupper Africa's chances of escaping from its plight.

The form of Africa's failure has been wholly defined by the famous Lomé–Cotonou accords linking sub-Saharan Africa to the European Union. These perpetuated the old division of labour by relegating independent Africa to the production of raw materials, at the very time (1955–75) when the third world was elsewhere embarking upon the industrial revolution. The accords therefore made Africa lose thirty years at a decisive moment of historical change. It is true that the African ruling classes had a share of responsibility for the decades of waste, especially when they lined up in the neocolonial camp against the aspirations of their own peoples and exploited their weaknesses.

So, the complicity of African ruling classes with the global strategies of imperialism was the ultimate cause of failure. We find again here, in this complicity, all the concerns underlying the geostrategic and other dimensions of imperialist strategy in the postwar period (1945–90), when the USSR was seeking to ally itself with African liberation movements, especially the more radical ones in Angola, Mozambique, Zimbabwe and South Africa, and when the Western powers responded by supporting, almost unconditionally, the most corrupt regimes imaginable. At the point we have reached today, Africa no longer counts in the calculations of the Western powers except as a source of oil and minerals – hence Washington's drive to control the oil regions in the Gulf of Guinea, from Senegal to Angola, which are closer and less vulnerable than those of the Middle East. Of course, the strategy to achieve this end exploits and manipulates, with shameless cynicism, the ethnicist and other tragic delusions of peoples with their backs to the wall.

It is now programmed in advance that the exclusion of Africa, in the sense of Africa's peoples, will make it possible for the continent to be included in the global system of natural resources.

Is South Africa the weak link in the system?

Africa south of the Sahara has a single modern, industrialized country: the Republic of South Africa. The victory of its black population, which put an end to apartheid, was accordingly hailed as the beginning of a possible 'rebirth' for the whole continent. How do things really stand in this respect?

South Africa is not easy to place in any of the usual categories: it is a kind of microcosm of the world capitalist system, which brings together in a single territory a number of features peculiar to each constituent category of that system. It has a white population which, in its lifestyle and standard of living, belongs to the 'first world', while the urban areas reserved for blacks and coloureds belong to the modern industrial 'third world', and the Bantustans (now ex-Bantustans!) containing the 'tribal' peasantry do not differ from peasant communities in Africa's 'fourth world'.

Originally, the Dutch settlers wanted to create a colony of their own and considered the Africans to be unwanted intruders. But then British imperialism, which had an interest in the country's mineral wealth, understood that a black workforce would be the least costly solution – and it came about that the British, not the Boers, invented apartheid at the end of the nineteenth century. To be more precise, they created a number of overpopulated 'native reservations' within the Union, and two others as the protectorates of Basutoland and Swaziland, which lacked the capacity to support their population in the absence of any investment to step up food production. The deliberate result was that workers living in these reservations were forced to supply the manpower needed for the mines.

In the aftermath of the Second World War, the Boers took charge of running this system, gave it a name (apartheid) and systematized the racist practices codified in the law. Over the next half-century, the ruling class pursued its project of climbing higher in the world system by means of state-protected and state-supported industrialization. Apartheid suited this project down to the ground. For a cheap workforce did not necessarily create a problem of output markets: it was possible to generate demand by distributing high incomes to an unproductive, or less productive, minority, and by boosting exports to cover the imports required for an efficient industry. The liberal rhetoric which claimed that apartheid conflicted with capitalism failed to address the real question.

The success or failure of capitalist industrialization can be measured by its 'competitiveness' on the world market. From this point of view, the countries of the periphery fall into one of three categories. A first group comprises industrial countries that have managed to become competitive, or at least could become competitive through relatively minor adjustments: the countries of Asia, communist or capitalist, and some of the major Latin American countries, especially Brazil. A second group, including South Africa, Egypt and Algeria, consists of industrial countries that have not become competitive, and that, in order to achieve this, would have radically to restructure their productive system and income distribution. A third group still remains at a pre-industrial stage, where economic growth, if any, is based on exports of primary products (agricultural goods, oil and minerals). Only the countries of the first group form the core of the modern periphery.

South Africa presents the curious picture of a country on whose territory features typical of each of these categories coexist with one another. Its industry is not competitive, and so its (non-mineral) industrial exports find their way abroad with difficulty, and only in the direction of captive markets. From the point of view of the global system, South Africa is little more than an exporter of primary products. The page of apartheid has turned, but this victory is only a first step on the long road that the country must travel to erase the ignoble legacy of its historical formation. The failure of apartheid to build a competitive industry should be explained in terms of the effective workplace and township struggles of the black working class, as well as the political capability of its mass organizations (ANC, Communist Party, COSATU trade unions). This failure was compounded by the mindless waste associated with the apartheid system, especially the gross overpayment of unproductive whites.

The compromise that brought apartheid to an end allowed for only limited forms of 'democratization'. The black majority did not inherit a prosperous country whose structures required no more than minor reforms, and in the event the black working class was asked to speed up the march to 'competitiveness'. In other words, it was supposed to accomplish for the sake of capital what capitalism had been unable to achieve with the active support of the West. The idea was that the necessary zeal could be purchased through concessions to industrial workers alone, while next to nothing would be done to improve the lot of the destitute peasantry in the ex-Bantustans, and the economic privileges of the parasitic minority would be preserved.

The post-apartheid compromise also ruled out an agrarian reform, so that no landowner could be forced to surrender, or even to sell, his land at a price less than he asked for it. The African majority put on a brave face and swallowed this restriction, in the belief that land reform was no longer one of the demands on the progressive agenda; it seemed a better idea to speed up modernization of the inherited agricultural system, particularly by opening it up to agribusiness and 'competitiveness', rather than try to re-create a 'pre-modern' peasantry. This reasoning would have made sense only if industrial expansion and urbanization were capable of giving work to everyone. But that is not the case: the modernization of industry, itself subject to the demands of 'competitiveness', leads in the end to massive redundancies. The reservations have become 'dumping areas' for the system's new poor, and it is impossible to start up there any agricultural activity worthy of the name. An agrarian reform has therefore become more necessary than ever. The Communist Party has started to change its line on the question and to mobilize the 'landless', whose clamorous demands, echoing recent events in Zimbabwe, are a crushing rebuke to ANC leaders who claim that 'there is no demand for land reform'. But the basic law still allows 'restitution' only to people who can prove before a court that their land was 'stolen' from them or their ancestors. This Anglo-Saxon notion, stemming from so-called egalitarian justice à la Rawls, fails to appreciate that social justice has to be established here and now, for the benefit of victims of the system, regardless of any 'inherited' rights of real or mythical ancestors.

The alternative entails a genuine democracy capable of sustaining profound social transformations. This is a huge agenda for the next thirty to fifty years, which will require serious effort to develop backward rural areas, together with a long-term perspective of internal redistribution of the population. Land reform and the promotion of black family farms will be necessary in areas occupied by white farmers: the much-trumpeted 'success' of white agriculture in South Africa has been based on exploitation of an underpaid workforce and wastage of natural resources (the land). At the same time, there will be a need to redistribute incomes in favour of wage-earners in the black majority and to improve their living conditions, especially in the fields of health and education; this will require cuts in the cost of maintaining large numbers of unproductive individuals in the white minority. For these objectives to be attained, it will be essential to restructure the modern industrial sector – which is out of the question if the main priority is to become a 'competitive' exporter in the shortest possible time. Whether one likes it or not, the political economy of genuine democratization entails a process of what I call 'delinking'.

South Africa today is not heading towards this kind of alternative reconstruction. Everything is being done to 'maintain' the legacy – 'reinforcing the mould', as Hein Marais put it. Popular struggles, which are therefore bound to intensify, mean that the country will remain a 'weak link' (as Langa Zita has written) in the new system of capitalist globalization.

Can the slide of the Arab world be reversed?

The Arab world shows signs of what we should call 'failed international insertion' – in comparison, that is, with the countries of East and South Asia or Latin America, whose visible levels of development (degree of industrialization and urbanization) are of the same order. This failure is economic: the industries in question are scarcely competitive on the world market, and agricultural output and food production are often in decline. But it is also political: the Arab states are turning their back on the tendencies to democratization apparent elsewhere, and the Arab peoples seem to be largely carried along by (illusory) hopes in an 'Islamic solution' to their problems.

One might, of course, simply explain this dramatic drift by the socially disastrous submission to the exigencies of neoliberal globalization (structural adjustment and uncontrolled *infitah*, or opening). But the fact remains that, in a previous period of contemporary history, the Arab world kept abreast of the Bandung struggles, while the national-populist regimes, initially both popular and legitimate, had a number of real achievements to their credit. These advances crowned an early awareness of the challenges of modernization, which had first appeared in the nineteenth century with Mohamed Ali in Egypt and the *Nahda*, or renaissance, of the second half of the century. The sudden end to this evolution, indeed its reversal in favour of obscurantist yearnings, presents a real problem for analysis.

A correct answer cannot be given without a deeper critical reading of the formation of the Arab world and its dominant religion, Islam. The challenge currently posed by the geopolitics of imperialism cannot be successfully taken up unless the Arab peoples are able to develop and impose the kind of multidimensional transformations within their own society that they are certainly not addressing today.

The present drift of the Arab world has its roots in the failure of the nineteenth-century *Nahda* and the limits of the national-populist phase. In keeping with this analysis, I have already elsewhere made a critique of political Islam and its claim to meet the challenge, and tried to show that it has been taking the peoples in question into a dead end. This political Islam is not a 'religious movement', and so attempts to analyse it in the context of theological debates fall wide of the mark. It is a political movement that mobilizes (and manipulates) 'religious feelings' in the struggle for power. Political Islam presents itself as 'radically anti-Western' (as well as 'anti-European' or even 'anti-Christian'), but never as anti-capitalist. For a further discussion of these complex matters, I can do no more here than refer the reader to texts which, even if I tried briefly to summarize them, would take us a long way from the main theme of this work.

To repeat, the conclusion to be drawn from the evolution of the Arab countries over the last twenty-five years is that they have failed actively to insert themselves into the world capitalist system. Moves in this direction were made in the previous period of nationalist resurgence, through incipient industrialization and state modernization based on sweeping social changes (land reform, educational progress, etc.) that both reduced income inequality and enlarged the middle layers of society, thereby achieving greater social cohesion and wider acceptance of the modernization project. Active state intervention – with nationalizations as its most advanced expression – served key functions in this project of 'catching up within a framework of negotiated interdependence'; we may even say that it was the sine qua non for implementation of that project.

Of course, the project itself was by no means free of serious internal contradictions, which limited its scope and exhausted its potential more rapidly than most people expected at the time. Indeed, the historical limits of the whole project were expressed in the populist methods of running the political system, in depoliticization of the popular classes and denial of their right to organization and independent initiative, in the closure of debate on ideological and cultural issues (especially the relationship between state and religion) that had shaped divisions both within the right ('feudal' versus 'liberal') and between the right and the Marxist or nationalist left in the decades since the *Nahda*: in short, the historical limits were expressed in the lack of democratization of society and politics.

Arab nationalism, which originally took shape as a national project within each of the Arab states (*qutri* in Arabic), only gradually became aware of its unitary, pan-Arab dimension (*qawmi* in Arabic), although it is true that in the Fertile Crescent this had more ancient roots. But the unitary perspective – which would obviously have solved many problems and put new life into the pursuit of development – never managed to become dominant, even in the Maghreb or the Fertile Crescent, because it continued to be based on the undemocratic principle of unity through conquest starting from a 'base province' under a single charismatic figure. This conception of conquest–liberation derived its legitimacy and its claim to be effective from the postulate of a pre-existing Arab nation, which merely awaited a liberator to assert its existence. It should be added that this national-bourgeois Arab project was also systematically combated by the dominant external forces – the imperialist powers. The alliance that the Arab national movement made with the Soviet Union was not at all the reason for this hostility, but a response to it. For the Western powers feared above all that a modernized unitary Arab state on the southern flank of Europe, rich in oil resources, would establish itself as a force to be reckoned with in the world system. This is why Israel was mobilized as a military instrument of permanent aggression, playing a major role in the overthrow of Arab nationalist regimes.

It is geostrategic considerations which explain the hostility of the Western powers to the bourgeoisies of the Arab world; the importance of the region had to do with its oil wealth and its position on the southern flank of the Soviet Union. Thus, Western strategies also had a share of responsibility for the Arab failure. (By contrast, geostrategic considerations compelled the Western imperialists to support, or to tolerate, the initiatives of the bourgeoisies of East Asia – which at least partly accounts for the region's successes in the period of postwar capitalist expansion.) We should remember that, shortly after Bandung, the United States mobilized its loyal allies in the region – Saudi Arabia and Pakistan – and began the process of setting up the 'Islamic Conference', with the aim of dividing the peoples of Asia and Africa on a religious basis, as the Non-Aligned Movement of the time perfectly understood. The 'Conference' would come to be the harbour from which the political Islamic movement was launched.

Be this as it may, the page of populist nationalism has turned. Liberal discourse claims that new policies of economic openness have put an end to the 'bad old ways', making it possible for real, 'healthy' development to take off. The reality is the exact opposite: such policies have broken the momentum of development, fragmented the Arab world and sharpened the rivalries within it, eventually plunging the region into a social disaster and wiping out its potential for rebirth.

Recompradorization of the Arab countries, which is the real aim of triad strategy, involves different economic, political and strategic dimensions. It is intended to break up the Arab region into three sub-regions, each subject to a distinctive comprador logic.

The Gulf oil region, separated from the rest of the Arab world and placed under US military tutelage, has lost all margin for autonomous political or financial action. The countries of the Maghreb have been left to the hazards of an eventual negotiation of their relations with Europe, so that one can speak there only of extremely vague projects for the future. The Arab Mashreq, for its part, is the object of an ongoing US–Israeli 'Middle East project' to create a totally integrated economy with three partners: Israel, the Occupied Territories (planned to be a kind of non-sovereign Bantustan) and Jordan, to which Lebanon, Syria and Egypt can be added later on. The idea, then, is to create an area for Israeli economic expansion, protecting Israeli exports from the competition of countries much more competitive on world markets. The Madrid and Oslo accords on the future of the Occupied Territories and Arab–Israeli peace are interpreted unilaterally, in a way that contradicts UN resolutions concerning a Palestinian state and the right of return of refugees, even though the principles behind those resolutions were reaffirmed in the accords themselves. The aim of the policies in operation is to consolidate the Bantustan status that the Israeli military authorities have systematically fostered in the Occupied Territories, by destroying productive activity there through the denial of access to water for agriculture, the requisitioning of land, the demolition of villages, the imposition of additional taxes on economic activity, the physical destruction of transport infrastructure and social services, and so on. By these means the occupation authorities have compelled the active Arab population to turn itself en masse into migrant day labourers, thereby providing the Israeli economy with a cheap supply of labour. Politically, the US–Israeli project does not envisage a sovereign Palestinian state that is master of its customs, taxation and monetary policy. Nor does it recognize the right of return for Palestinian refugees that has been reaffirmed in United Nations resolutions.

Whatever else one might say of it, this remains a fragile project, if only because the struggle of the Palestinian people will continue as long as its legitimate rights are not recognized. The project further marginalizes Egypt within the region and the Arab world, and there is nothing to say that the Egyptian regime will accept this indefinitely. The American project for the Arab world also leaves unanswered such important questions as the future of Iraq or the place and role of Turkey and Iran in the region. Nor does it concern itself with the Arab 'fourth world' (Mauritania, Sudan, Somalia and Yemen), which for the time being is totally marginalized.

The various projects put forward in the name of economic liberalism never set the goal of halting the slide of the Arab world, any more than short-term crisis management policies have sought to do elsewhere. The point was not to establish a new world order safe from crisis. Moreover, the prosperity of the years of oil plenty (1973–84) was based on the illusion of consumption; the opportunity was not taken to strengthen the productive base. It is true that the illusion served the crucial political function of giving the *infitah* a semblance of legitimacy and winning broad public support. But, as one would have expected, this all proved to be short-lived. The United States went back on the offensive, reduced the Gulf states to the status of military protectorates, held hostage the fortunes they had placed on the finance markets, and imposed a devastating blockade on Libya. The economic regression resulting from these crisis management policies made the whole Arab world a candidate for 'fourth worldization': that is, marginalization within the world system, alongside sub-Saharan African and a number of Asian countries (Afghanistan, Pakistan and Bangladesh).

Latin America and the Caribbean
in a tricontinental perspective

All the countries of modern ('post-Columbian') America share a number of characteristics inherited from the years of their formation. Shaped by mercantilist Atlantic Europe as a periphery of capitalism, then settled by waves of immigrants in the nineteenth and twentieth centuries, Latin America is certainly a different continent from Asia and Africa.

With the end of mercantilism, the fate of the independent Americas was bound to diverge. The United States, a new capitalist-imperialist centre, announced in the Monroe doctrine (1823) that it intended to keep the rest of the continent as a periphery for its own benefit. This asymmetry has grown deeper in the course of the last two centuries, through solid class alliances among the dominant agrarian oligarchies of the South and the expansion of small-scale local capitalism, in association with inward migration and the (European, then North American) capital of globally dominant oligopolies. The resulting social structures are marked both by huge inequalities (the most violent ever known) and by forms of colonial subjugation of the 'natives' (Mexican and Andean Indians) and descendants of black slaves.

The peoples of the continent have certainly never accepted the wretched lot that the dominant local classes reserved for them, and their struggles and revolts fill the history of the past two centuries. Fractions of the educated and enlightened classes have rejected Washington's yoke, and when they have forged links of solidarity with their peoples this has yielded powerful episodes of anti-imperialist struggle, with a potential to develop in an anti-capitalist direction. The revolutions in Mexico (1910–20) and Cuba, together with 'social-democratic' experiments as in Allende's Chile, are the best illustrations of this history.

After the Second World War, Latin America invented a *desarrollista* or 'development' model that was in every respect analogous to that of the non-aligned countries in Asia and Africa. Very early on, the so-called 'dependency school' on the left subjected this model to trenchant theoretical criticism, which also lent legitimacy to the armed struggles of the Guevarist period. We now have from Marta Harnecker a magnificent analysis of the history of the last fifty years. The peoples and vanguards of Latin America eventually drew closer to the Asia and Africa of Bandung. But, whereas there the anti-imperialist project of liberation and development was shared by both governments (following the victory of liberation movements) and peoples, the governments of Latin America held firm as opponents of the movement and loyal subordinate allies of Washington. Cuba was the exception, the only state that joined the camp of the non-aligned. The Tricontinental, established in Havana soon after the victory of the revolution, was a front of the peoples, represented by their revolutionary organizations rather than their governments.

By the end of the 1970s the *desarrollista* model was exhausted, and so too, for the same reasons, was the Bandung model of national populism. But since in Latin America the final stages of that model had been largely associated with violent military dictatorships (supported and legitimized by the imperialist powers), its demise brought on the fall of the dictatorships in question. Hence the ambiguity of the legacy: democracy associated with the triumph of neoliberal globalization. As we know, the social catastrophes to which this led served to devalue, in the eyes of the popular classes, the option of restricted multiparty democracy and electoralism. Yet the peoples of Latin America began to raise significantly their awareness of the true challenges facing them: evidence of this are the neo-Zapatista movement in Mexico, the electoral victory of the Workers Party and Lula in Brazil, the rise of Chávez in Venezuela; the evolution of Kirchner's Argentina; and events in Bolivia and Ecuador. Nor is it an accident that moves were made to draw closer to Asia and Africa, perhaps under the initial impetus of the Group of 20 (led by Brazil, South Africa, China and India) within the WTO.

The challenge facing the peoples of Latin America remains huge. It is multidimensional: political and social, internal and external. Taking it up requires simultaneous advances in three interlinked directions: the extension of democracy to the realms of economic and social management; guarantees of social progress for the dominated classes and a reduction in inequalities; and a strengthening of national independence in the face of Washington's drive for mastery. Until now, modern Latin America has never devised and implemented strategies to permit this threefold concomitant advance. In the 1940s and 1950s, populist experiments, beginning with Perón but emulated in Brazil and elsewhere, did achieve a number of social advances (most marked in Argentina, weaker in other countries), but these were always implemented from the top down, without democracy. There were times when a will to independence, to 'control over foreign capital', asserted itself – and military regimes were sometimes, by no means always, at the head of this. There were also a number of democratic advances, though at the price of social stagnation or even a worsening of social conditions, and always with a weakening assertion of national autonomy. In Brazil F.H. Cardoso symbolized this option better than anyone else. Will Lula's Brazil and Chávez's Venezuela, pulling others in their wake, be capable of facing up to the challenge and making (perhaps initially modest) advances in the above three directions?

In Latin America, as elsewhere, the internal and external dimensions of the challenge are inseparably bound up with each other. There will be no genuine multipolarity unless the relevant partners embark upon social changes, and such changes will in turn require that society frees itself from the grip of neoliberalism.

The East as a new South?

In previous chapters, I have dealt with only one former Eastern bloc country that went over to out-and-out capitalism: Russia. And, in the first chapter (on the triad), I put forward an argument about the 'real Europe' whose frontiers stopped in eastern Germany, as opposed to the new members and candidate members of the European Union.

My choice was deliberate. For the de facto course of the West European powers is bound to lead to a kind of 'Latin Americanization' elsewhere in the continent: that is, with the EU as it exists today, the relationship between the economies of 'developed' capitalist Europe and those of eastern and south-eastern Europe will on every point be analogous to the relationship between the United States and Latin America, an asymmetrical relationship involving subordination of the weak. In one sense, the European Union functions in the same way that the planned expansion of NAFTA (North American Free Trade Agreement) is meant to achieve for the whole continent from Alaska to Tierra del Fuego – in terms of content, of course, independently of the institutional forms peculiar to the two regions in question, perhaps even of their different 'intentions' (which may thus be no more than illusions). For the 'opening of the market' in eastern Europe will produce nothing other than a serious deterioration of its social situation.

It is evidently important to discuss both the possible public reactions in eastern Europe to this new challenge and the changes that would be desirable in the European project to address it correctly.

A new basis for solidarity among the peoples of the South

A new comprador structure is now in the offing for all the peripheries of the world system, but this 'recompradorization' is operating on terrains that the uneven results of the Bandung project have made different from one another. Structural adjustment, as it is conceived in the framework of neoliberal globalization, is simply unilateral adjustment of the peripheries to the exigencies of global expansion for the benefit of core capital. What we need, however, are mutual adjustments among the great, unevenly developed regions of the world, adjustments based on collective negotiation that makes global interdependence fit the requirements of national and regional strategies, while taking into account the inequalities inherited from polarization.

Adjustment processes that comply with the dominant logic of the system create the political conditions to perpetuate inherited inequalities. In the richest countries of the third world, they strengthen the positions of a comprador bourgeoisie that actually benefits from its insertion into globalized capitalism; while in the fourth world (where such strengthening is scarcely an issue) they still create conditions that work against the crystallization of adequate popular responses. These negative tendencies then fuel explosions that fit almost naturally into the fragmentation of the country, as it splits into ethnic or pseudo-ethnic regions produced by loss of state legitimacy and the shattering of the hitherto dominant social bloc. Africa already provides some examples of this kind of tragedy. But the more intense marginalization to which it leads is a tragedy only for the peoples concerned; it does not 'threaten the world order'.

There is an alternative, however, even if it remains difficult to assemble the conditions for it to succeed. First of all, at the base of society, it would be necessary to create a national, popular, democratic front worthy of the name. But that would in turn require genuinely multipolar tendencies to begin to emerge at the level of the world system, so as to reduce the constraints which, in the present state of the world, weigh with all their force against the crystallization of a democratic popular alternative.

Compradorization has largely discredited regimes geared to the requirements of neoliberal globalization. It follows that a 'remake' of Bandung, uniting peoples behind their governments, is today an illusory prospect. The solidarity that is needed today will have to be built primarily by the peoples themselves. Only then can hope be reborn, only then can governments be forced (or new governments created) to shake off the grip of neoliberalism and to lay the basis for a new active front of the South.

Although some countries in the South at least seem to be run in accordance with the principles of electoral democracy (no more than that), many others are not really democratic, to say the least, or are quite frankly appalling. Authoritarian structures here favour comprador fractions whose interests are bound up with the expansion of global imperialist capitalism.

The alternative – the construction of a front among the peoples of the South – will therefore have to involve democratization. It will be a long and difficult process, but it surely cannot be helped by the installation of puppet regimes that hand over their country's wealth to rapacious North American transnationals, since – apart from anything else – such regimes will be still no less fragile, credible and legitimate than the ones they replace under the aegis of invading US forces. Besides, for all its hypocritical talk, Washington's objective is not to promote democracy in the world.

The key foundations for a broad alliance of solidarity among the peoples and states of the South

On the basis of certain positions taken by countries in the South, as well as certain ideas that are gaining ground there, we can now glimpse the broad outlines of a new 'front of the South'. The positions in question concern both the field of politics and the economic management of globalization.

At the political level: condemnation of the new US policy principle of 'preventive war', and demands for the removal of all foreign military bases in Asia, Africa and Latin America.

The regions chosen by Washington for its first assaults are the Arab Middle East (Iraq and Palestine, the latter via unconditional support for Israel), the Balkans (Yugoslavia, with a new US presence in Hungary, Romania and Bulgaria), Central Asia and the Caucasus (Afghanistan and parts of the former USSR). The achievement of US aims here requires the establishment of puppet regimes through US military action. From Beijing to Delhi and Moscow, it is becoming ever clearer that wars 'made in the USA' are a threat directed more against China, Russia and India than against their immediate victims, such as Iraq.

A return to the Bandung position of no military bases in Asia or Africa is now on the agenda, even if, under present circumstances, the non-aligned countries have agreed to remain silent over the American protectorates in the Gulf. In this respect, the non-aligned countries have taken positions close to the ones defended by France and Germany at the UN Security Council, thereby helping to underline the diplomatic and moral isolation of the aggressor.

The question of the foreign bases, and the military threat they pose, does not concern Asia and Africa alone. The Brazilian Amazon is also the object of covetous gazes – which is why the permanent US military presence in Colombia is certainly a source of concern in Brasilia. The threats against Cuba, and Washington's arrogant posture in its Caribbean 'backyard' and in Venezuela, are a further reason to give substance to the demands of the countries of the South.

With regard to economic management of the world system, the interests of all the countries in the South are convergent and we can again see the broad outlines of an alternative that they might collectively champion.

1. The idea of controls on international capital transfers is making a comeback. In fact, the 'liberalization' of capital accounts, which the IMF imposes as a new dogma, has no other purpose than to facilitate the massive transfer of capital to the United States, to cover a growing American deficit due to problems in the US economy itself as well as the costs of its strategy of global military control. The countries of the South have no interest in making it easier for their capital to drain away or for speculative raids to wreak havoc with their economy. They should therefore question their submission to all the vagaries

of 'flexible exchange rates', which is a logical sequel to the demand for the opening of capital accounts. Instead, the establishment of region-wide systems to stabilize exchange rates should be a theme of systematic research and debate within the Non-Aligned Movement and the Group of 77. Already in 1997, against the background of the Asian financial crisis, Malaysia took the initiative of restoring exchange controls and won the ensuing battle; the IMF itself was forced to recognize them.

2. The idea of foreign investment regulation is making a comeback. Third world countries clearly do not think, as some did in the past, that they should close their doors to all foreign investment. Indeed, they actually call for an increase in direct investment. But the forms in which it is received are again the object of critical reflection to which some governments in the third world are themselves not insensitive. In close connection with this issue, there is now considerable doubt about the model of intellectual and industrial property rights that the WTO is seeking to impose, since it has become clear that, far from favouring 'transparent' competition in open markets, it is actually designed to strengthen the monopoly position of transnational corporations.

3. Many countries in the South again realize that they cannot dispense with an agricultural development policy – one that will help them achieve national food security and prevent their peasantry from disintegrating under the impact of WTO-driven 'competition'. In reality, the opening of agricultural product markets – which enables the USA, Europe and a handful of countries in the South (above all the Southern Cone) to export their surpluses to the third world – threatens the goal of national food security without offering anything in return, since the output of third world peasant producers continues to face insurmountable obstacles in the markets of the North. The neoliberal strategy that is breaking up the peasantry and hastening its migration to the shanty towns has therefore triggered the reappearance of peasant struggles and sown alarm among the local regimes.

In the WTO, in particular, discussions of agriculture tend to focus exclusively on EU or US support for farmers and export subsidies. This fixation on world trade in agricultural products simply leaves out of the picture the major preoccupations with which we have been dealing. It also involves some curious ambiguities, since it calls on countries in the South to adopt even more liberal positions than those actually implemented by governments in the North – much to the delight of the World Bank (which is hardly known for defending the interests of the South). EU or US support for its own farmers is one thing – and, after all, if we defend the principle of a distribution of income in the South, there is no reason why the countries of the North should not have the same right! But this should be kept separate from the quite different issue of subsidies to support the overseas dumping of the North's agricultural products.

4. The external debt is no longer felt to be only economically unbearable; its very legitimacy is beginning to be questioned. Demands are being raised for unilateral repudiation of the odious and illegitimate debts, and for moves towards proper international legislation on debt, such as does not exist today. A general audit would doubtless uncover a significant proportion of illegitimate, in some cases straightforwardly criminal, forms of debt. Interest payments alone have reached such levels that the (legally founded) demand for their reimbursement would effectively wipe out the present debt and show the whole operation to have been a primitive form of pillage. To achieve this, the idea of normal civilized legislation to regulate external debt, along the same lines as internal debt, should become the subject of a special campaign, within a wider perspective of advancing international law and strengthening its legitimacy. As we know, it is precisely because the law is silent in this domain that such matters are resolved through a trial of brute strength. The prevailing relationship of forces thus makes it possible to present as legitimate international debts which, if debtor and creditor belonged to the same nation and the same system of laws, would land them both in the courts on a charge of criminal conspiracy.

Lastly, questions concerning cultural diversity should be discussed in the framework of the new international perspectives outlined above. Now, cultural diversity is a fact of life, but a complex and ambiguous fact. Diversities inherited from the past, however legitimate, are not necessarily on a par with that diversity in the construction of the future which should be not only accepted but actively sought out. To conjure up only inherited diversity (political Islam, Hindutva, Confucianism, *négritude*, chauvinistic ethnicity) is often a demagogic exercise on the part of autocratic or comprador regimes, which enables them both to dispel the challenge of universal civilization and to bow in practice before the dictates of transnational capital. Moreover, exclusive insistence on such legacies divides the third world, by opposing to one another political Islam and Hindutva in Asia, or Muslims, Christians and other religious believers in Africa. The recasting of a united political front of the South is the way to overcome these divisions supported by American imperialism. But what needs to be done to advance genuinely universal concepts, enriched with the contributions of one and all? The debate on this cannot be ignored.

CHAPTER 6

Reform of the UN as a part of multipolar globalization

The ruling classes of the triad consider that the United Nations has 'had its day' and have substituted for it the G8 and Nato, thereby revoking the functions of the General Assembly. What is involved is a real *coup de force*, a negation of the sovereignty of states (or, to be more precise, of the South) and even of international law. If the triad states persist in this course, the 'multipolar' concepts that they now and again support will express a mere wish to 'rebalance Atlanticism', nothing more.

Genuine multipolarity means a commitment to different principles: respect for national sovereignty and international law. It is true that the ideas underlying them deserve to be reviewed, not because of the requirements of neoliberal globalization but, on the contrary, to carry the ideas further and to make them fit better with the requirements of democratization in all societies on earth. Such a review therefore entails strengthening, not weakening, the institutional framework, including primarily the United Nations.

Managing national sovereignty within the UN framework

The United Nations came into being during a long historical period in which there was a close match between management of the economy and management of politics. As we shall see, this match – a product of capitalist modernization – was a characteristic feature of mature capitalism, a kind of late crowning, but today the evolution of the system is calling it into question. The philosophy of the world system rests in fact upon two principles: the absolute sovereignty of states (considered as 'nation-states' by nature) and polycentrism.

The Treaty of Westphalia (1648), which ushered in this system, related specifically only to the area of the old world of Catholicism, whose unity had been blown apart by the Reformation. Extended to the rest of Europe through the Treaty of Vienna (1815), it went through a first, partial universalization with the creation of the League of Nations (1920).

The Second World War ended with the victory of democracy over fascism, and of the peoples of Africa and Asia over colonialism. The creation of the United Nations took place within this atmosphere.

This dual victory governed the economic, social and political forms of system management, both nationally and at the level of international organization. It laid the basis for the three fundamental 'historic compromises' of the time: the welfare state in the West (a compromise between labour and capital made possible as the working classes won a dignity unknown in earlier stages of capitalism); 'actually existing socialism'; and what I call the national populism of the newly liberated countries of Asia and Africa.

The dual victory also paved the way for negotiated political management of international relations, thereby promoting the role of the United Nations. Today it is considered good form to say that Cold War bipolarism and the veto powers of the five permanent members of the Security Council (in practice, only of the two superpowers) paralysed the United Nations. In fact, the opposite was the case: the veto-backed bipolarism gave countries on the periphery of the system (Asia, Africa, Latin America) a room for manoeuvre that they have since lost. For a time, the core imperialist countries were forced to adapt to demands that they should respect the sovereignty of the peoples in question, and to accept (or play along with) their plans for national and social development. During the Bandung period (1955–75), the permanent imperialist tendency of actually existing capitalism was, if not radically called into question, then at least toned down. Not by chance did the rise, and the glorious period, of the United Nations occur at this time.

The spirit of the United Nations Charter commands a polycentric vision of globalization. By this I mean forms of globalization based on the principle of negotiation, as the only guarantee of genuine respect for diversity in all its dimensions: cultural and linguistic, to be sure, but also those which have historically resulted from the inequalities of economic development. Polycentrism respects all states, all nations, both large and small; it accepts that, in a way, each is a centre unto itself, and that the interdependence involved in globalization must therefore be able to get along with the legitimate demands built into the 'auto-centred' visions of all its partners. Globalization must therefore be 'negotiated' and, though not perfectly equal, must at least be conceived in such as a way as to reduce inequalities, not to make them deeper. To reconcile existing differences with the universal requirements of peace, democracy and development: this is the challenge.

The international order that came into being with the creation of the United Nations in 1945 was based upon three complementary principles: respect for the sovereignty of states, a ban on war, and a ban on interference in the internal affairs of member states.

In the old League of Nations, the principle of state sovereignty had not been extended to 'all nations'; colonial rule was still considered normal for some of them. Similarly, the League of Nations did not formally prohibit recourse to war. If the United Nations Charter enlarged the scope of these principles, it was precisely because they had been trampled on by the fascist powers. Following the victory in 1945, it was therefore logical to strengthen the principle by prohibiting recourse to war: individual states were permitted to defend themselves against any power that infringed their sovereignty through aggression, but they were condemned out of hand if they were themselves the aggressor. All conflicts between states were to be resolved by the political means of negotiation, if possible under the auspices of the United Nations. Only the UN Security Council had the authority, if the need arose, to organize a military intervention, and this had to be both proportionate and limited in time. Over the following decades, moreover, the recognition of sovereignty was extended to all nations in the world, and the idea of colonial rule was condemned without reservation.

Within this framework, the settlement of inter-state disputes was still the exclusive responsibility of states; the 'peoples' in question (whether as individuals or organizations) could not claim rights that were denied them. This was, and still is, the status of the court in the Hague. The idea of an international court of justice for certain types of crime (war crimes, crimes against humanity, genocide) has only recently taken shape, and is still rejected by the main world power and a few other countries.

Thus, sovereignty continued to be interpreted in an absolute sense, to prohibit any country from 'interfering in the internal affairs' of another; nations were represented by their governments so long as these gave the appearance of governing stably. The world order implied a vision in which human rights were purely an internal affair. The UN declaration that formulated these rights had no juridical value and lacked any supranational jurisdiction to enforce them. Only Europe, in later years, went further and created embryos of European courts.

Basic social rights to life, food, education, health, social security and work, as well as workers' rights, remained entirely a matter for national legislation. At the demand of third world countries (the Group of 77 and the group of non-aligned countries), certain economic and social rights to development were introduced into a general, rather vague UN declaration, which fitted more into the national-populist conception of development prevalent in the 1960s and 1970s than into a genuinely democratic project for multilateral adjustment on a world scale.

This whole legal system, with its basic concepts and standard practices, shows that the demand for democracy was not a major priority in itself for the dominant ideologies of the time. Although the advance of democracy was considered a praiseworthy objective, it was subordinate to the main goal of economic development. This view prevailed in the countries of Africa and Asia, where it legitimized single-party regimes (both socialist and others, as in Ivory Coast, Kenya, Malawi or Zaire). But it also permeated the Latin American ideology of *desarrollismo*. It was regarded as legitimate at an international level and in 'public opinion'. And it underpinned government policies and the practices of aid agencies, which at the time never tied their action to the kind of 'democratic conditions' with which we have since become familiar.

A balance sheet of UN activity between 1945 and 1980

It is scarcely surprising, therefore, that the heyday of the United Nations came at just this time – the rather brief period from the 1960s to 1975 or 1980 that coincided with what are called the 'development decades'. The ensuing questioning and crisis related not to the UN as such but to the world system in which it was inserted.

It is not difficult to draw a (positive) balance sheet of the period: the highest economic growth rates of modern times; huge social advances, in the core countries of the system and 'actually existing socialism', as well as in the great majority of countries in the liberated periphery; a flowering of new, proud and modern national identities.

The United Nations gave support to these radical changes and made it easier for them to succeed. At a political level, the dual principle of national sovereignty and polycentrism prohibited the kind of brutal intervention that had previously been the normal practice of imperialist powers (and that has again become the normal practice since Nato gave itself the responsibility to make order prevail on earth). In terms of economic management, it established the principle of international negotiation and left national states free to organize their own systems of production and income distribution as they saw fit. No doubt 'pessimists' will point out that negotiations (within UNCTAD, for example) rarely led to more than declarations with no real practical effect. But states did remain sovereign internally, and therefore had real negotiating powers that were used in ways acceptable to their ruling classes.

With regard to the preservation of peace, the balance sheet of UN activity down to the Gulf War of 1991 is fairly positive. By giving legitimacy to the liberation wars against British, Dutch, French, Belgian and Portuguese colonialism, it supported the construction of polycentrism. By comparison with what followed, the period saw few 'civil wars'; and although, as always in history, some powers tried to take advantage of them by adding fuel to the flames, the UN system did not work in favour of their manoeuvres (as we saw in the case of the Biafra war). At times the UN may well have been manipulated (as in the Korean War) or neutralized (in the American war in Vietnam or the Soviet invasion of Afghanistan). As to the Palestinian question, the UN certainly legitimized the creation of Israel in highly dubious forms, by allowing the Zionists not to implement the planned partition, but it subsequently tried to check Tel Aviv's expansionist drive, condemned the tripartite aggression of 1956, and condemned, in Resolution 242, the occupation of Palestinian territories after 1967.

The annual meetings of the UN General Assembly were always a major event, closely followed by leading political figures throughout the world. So, although the positions expressed by various parties did not always make it possible to reach a positive compromise, all world leaders at least had to take them into account.

The United Nations did not die a natural death: it was murdered in 1990–91 by decision of the United States, with the support of its triad allies, which ended the responsibilities of the organization for the management of polycentrism and the preservation of peace. The UN was murdered when Washington decided to implement its project of spreading the Monroe doctrine to the whole planet.

It is not difficult either to identify the limits of the UN system: its illusions concerning development and its democratic deficit. The concepts of economic and social development rested on the paradigms of the time, involving an overlap between management of the economy and the exercise of political power. 'Economic development' fitted into a 'catching up' logic of capitalist expansion, which in turn presupposed the neutrality of technology and the reproduction of hierarchical forms of organization generated by the history of capitalism. The fact that this model always implied at least some active role for a regulatory state (sometimes as replacement for a missing, or compradorized, capitalist class), and the fact that here and there the state took on certain social dimensions, do not mean that it had the socialist quality often too rashly conferred upon it. (For my own part, this is why I prefer to call it a national-populist state.)

Looking back on the period, it is right to stress the illusions nurtured by the successes of development, but it is surely not justifiable to instrumentalize that failure in the way that neoliberals consistently do. For what they subsequently imposed was the considerably more destructive illusion that deregulated capitalism would ensure 'better' development. The dogmatic rhetoric associated with this illusion has been refuted by the whole history of actually existing capitalism (even development in the limited sense of catching up, when it has taken place at all, has involved conflict with the dominant expansionary logic of globalized capital). It has been especially cruelly refuted by the stagnation tendencies of the last two decades (when development has gone by the board, to be replaced with ineffectual charity-talk about a 'war on poverty') and by the most scandalous aggravation of social injustices.

Another noteworthy point is that the system made no more than purely verbal references to democracy. Today, in different degrees, the world's peoples have become more demanding on this issue than they were in the age of the welfare state, actually existing socialism and populist nationalism. This is certainly a positive evolution, even if the democratic demands in question remain the object of sometimes easy manipulation on the part of the imperialist powers. In the thinking of that earlier age, individual states had absolute sovereignty as exclusive representatives of their peoples, and local ruling classes often justified the denial of democracy by invoking the necessities of 'national construction'.

When the world situation changed, slower economic growth put an end to the benefits enjoyed by broad layers of the population (especially the middle classes, but also the popular classes in so far as upward social mobility operated across generations). 'National' discourse then lost the legitimacy that had allowed it to skip over democratic rights, or even elementary human rights.

Finally, through its political action to protect national sovereignty and to support polycentrism, the United Nations helped to make it easier for the various post-war projects to be deployed. Although the political regimes that took responsibility for them were not democratic (or only very partially democratic), they were on the whole not as appalling as they are today often made out to have been. Modernizing, open to secularism and (with qualifications) the social advancement of women, these autocracies were often close to forms of 'enlightened despotism'. The most appalling regimes in those days were the ones that the imperialist enemy took every opportunity to instal or support: Mobutu in Zaire, Suharto in Indonesia, a series of South American dictatorships. Later history – such as the support for the obscurantist Taliban dictatorship in Afghanistan that succeeded an enlightened despotism too easily dismissed as 'communist' – testifies to the regression following the erosion of national populism.

For want of an objective balance-sheet of that period, the criticisms now levelled against UN activity are most often highly superficial – for example, in their emphasis on the 'mediocrity' of 'UN bureaucracies'. A calm comparison between the UN apparatuses and other national or multinational institutional systems (such as the EU's) would prompt more balanced conclusions.

Conflict and overlap between economic and political management

Since the space of social reproduction is always multidimensional – at once political, economic and cultural – the cohesion of a society depends on the extent to which these dimensions overlap with one another. Sometimes the overlap may operate at the level of a fairly large geographical area; sometimes fragmentation means that it has effect only at the level of micro-societies such as village communities. This does not exclude the possibility that contradictions and conflicts may emerge between the distinctive logics at various levels of the social reality in question; indeed, it is the unfurling of these contradictions which accounts for the dynamics of history and social change. Besides, the overlap is always relative, in the sense that the societies defined on the basis of it very rarely present an absolute or near-absolute autarky, but usually fit into wider 'systems of societies'. The areas of Christianity, Islam, Hinduism or Confucianism, for example, define cultural (religious or philosophical) dimensions common to whole sets of societies. We might similarly identify areas of market exchange that link together many different societies and make them more or less interdependent. In modern capitalism, the whole earth constitutes such an area, so that the economic side of social reproduction acquires the quality of a 'world economy'. But, in earlier times, one could speak of a number of huge areas of market exchange, such as those designated by the 'silk routes'.

In some regions, the clustering of interdependent human societies is so strong that their evident cohesion gives them a special identity. We may then speak of societies where there is an overlap between 'the market' (questionable shorthand for 'the economic dimension'), the state (the management of political power) and the society (which recognizes itself in a cultural identity).

Capitalism first triumphed in one particular region of the Old World – the north-western quarter, or less than a quarter, of Europe. It was an area where the conditions of both economic reproduction (largely reduced to self-supporting fiefdoms) and political management (largely reduced to the powers of the local lord) displayed a high degree of fragmentation. The broader regions into which the basic feudal units were inserted had a low density: a common 'Christendom' did not go together with real political power either at its apex (the Papacy) or at the level of the Holy Roman Emperor or the various monarchs. Market exchange had limited effects, and long-distance trade (along the 'silk routes', for example) predominated over local trade. For this reason, I use the term 'peripheral' to characterize this 'feudal' form of the 'tributary' societies of the epoch – in contrast to the core forms marked by an overlap of economy and political power, within considerably larger geographical areas. The early coagulation of new capitalist forms in these peripheries of the tributary world does not therefore seem to have been a matter of chance.

In a first period, when this new coagulation was taking place, the intensification of market exchange opened out into what I call the chaos of the origins of capitalism. The overlap between the spaces of political management and economic reproduction was shattered, as trade networks grew up alongside, and beyond, the ancient powers of feudal lords and the more limited ones of craft corporations. The map of Europe during this transition from the Middle Ages to the modern era looked like a veritable jigsaw of princedoms, *seigneuries* and semi-autonomous cities, each of them increasingly dependent on trade networks that eluded their powers. It is a model that contrasts with that of the central tributary worlds, where the subordination of market economy to the ruling powers was a major obstacle to the birth of thoroughly capitalist forms. The chaos was eventually overcome and a market/state (or economic/political) overlap rebuilt through the emergence of the modern nation-state. The United Provinces, but especially England and France (which invented the absolute monarchy of the *ancien régime*), paved the way for the full blossoming in the nineteenth century that became the model for the organization of the modern world.

The affirmation of sovereignty (of states, nations and peoples) is the result of this construction of capitalist modernity. A triple overlap among the spaces for capital accumulation management ('the market'), political management ('the state') and a distinctive cultural identity ('the nation') did indeed characterize the deployment of capitalism in its mature phase. Of course, this only applied to the major countries of the capitalist core, but it became the model for all the others and, curiously, also for the national liberation movements of the oppressed peoples and the revolutions made in the name of socialism. This affirmation found a late universalist expression, after the Second World War, and marked the history of the UN's glorious decades.

Today this model has entered a phase of final disintegration. There is a return to chaos, in conditions that present a new challenge of going beyond obsolescent capitalism.

The empire of chaos: sovereignty, social justice and development go by the board

Transformations of the productive system of contemporary capitalism are an incontrovertible fact, whether it is a question of the ongoing 'techno-logical revolutions' (computers, space, biotics) or their effects on the organization of work and social structures. A discussion of their scale and reach does not fall within the ambit of this book. But these new develop-ments pose a real challenge for all concepts relating to management of the capitalist world system: the respective functions of the 'market' and public intervention, the relations between democratic practices and social justice, the functions of international law and international institutions.

Should we conclude that the dominant forces give the 'right' answers to these new challenges, or anyway that 'there is no alternative' to them? That is certainly not my view. On the contrary, I argue that their an-swers are unacceptable, that they have thrown overboard both popular sovereignty and the prospects for people to develop in a context of social justice. Associated with the imbalance in the social and international relationship of forces, operating to the advantage of the dominant seg-ments of globalized capital, such answers – which inspire the liberal discourse of collective triad imperialism – are producing nothing other than an 'empire of chaos'. In doing this, they create the conditions for military globalization and give further encouragement to the hegemonist project of the United States.

The contemporary chaos is not analogous to that which presided over the dawn of capitalism. In its time, the past construction of the 'market/ state' overlap marked a real social advance accompanying the deployment of the higher capitalist mode. Today, capitalism has exhausted its progres-sive historical role and can offer no more than a barbaric downhill slide. This challenges us to think of a world beyond capitalism, and hence to focus our analysis on the conflict between the economy (the 'market' – that is, capitalism) and society beyond the state. It is a conflict that concerns every dimension of reality, both national and global.

Today we face a single project for the future, one that the dominant powers, themselves in the service of the dominant segments of globalized capital, are implementing by means of systematic violence, including military force. This project – the only possible one that accords with the immanent logic of capitalism at its present stage of development – has nothing in common with the 'liberal' vision of competitive and transparent rule by the market, of democracy promoted through 'civil society' instead of the 'bureaucratic', 'autocratic' state, of a world at peace provided only that the savage practices of 'terrorism' can be stamped out. It is the project of the dominant segments of globalized capital (the 'transnationals' of the imperialist triad). Elsewhere I have described the future it has in mind for humanity as 'apartheid on a world scale'. Permanent war against the peoples of Asia, Africa and Latin America is therefore inevitable if the project is to be successful – which means, of course, that the United Nations no longer has any role of its own to play: either it agrees to become a docile instrument of those running the permanent war against the South, or it has to disappear.

The project of American hegemonism fits into the liberal logic of collective triad imperialism. It entails that the 'sovereignty of US national interests' should be placed above all other principles framing the legitimacy of political action. To be sure, the imperialisms of the past behaved no differently, and those who seek to mitigate the responsibilities of the US establishment today, or to find excuses for its criminal conduct, frequently invoke the undeniable historical antecedents. But it is precisely here that one would have liked to see a change in history, the kind of change that was at least begun in 1945. It was because inter-imperialist conflict and fascist contempt for international law had produced the horrors of the Second World War that the United Nations was founded on a new principle that declared the illegitimacy of war. That fine initiative, however, which opened the way for the progress of civilization, never won the conviction of the ruling classes of the United States. Always ill at ease in the UN concert of nations, Washington today starkly spells out what it was previously forced to conceal: that it does not accept even the idea of an international law standing higher than what it considers necessary for the defence of US national interests. The United States is not alone responsible for the slide downhill. Europe played a large role of its own by adding fuel to the flames in Yugoslavia (through overhasty recognition of the independence of Croatia and Slovenia), then by rallying to Washington's positions on 'terrorism' and its war in Afghanistan. It remains to be seen whether Europe will begin to revise its stand following the war in Iraq. In any event, a return to the principle of polycentrism and a restored role for the UN will not be on the agenda so long as Europe agrees to substitute Nato for the United Nations as the means of managing globalization.

Washington's propaganda apparatus has been foretelling an inevitable 'clash of civilizations' (actually of religions) as the dominant feature of the future world. In reality, it has managed to give a real face to such a clash by a number of systematic measures: the promotion of various communalisms on the pretext of respecting difference; an offensive against 'outdated' secularism; praise for religious obscurantisms, which postmodernists have placed on a par with any other 'ideology'; systematic encouragement of nauseating ethnicist regimes (in the former Yugoslavia and elsewhere); various kinds of cynical manipulation (CIA support for terrorist groups against enemies of the USA, in Afghanistan, Chechnya and Algeria, among others); and a false and dishonest war on so-called 'terrorism' (where terror does not serve Washington's interests). The so-called clash of civilizations is an integral part of the barbaric downhill slide of capitalism; in no way is it an obstacle to the unfurling of the US hegemonist project.

Under these conditions, it is little surprise that peace and social justice, not to speak of development, have gone by the board – in spite of the noisy rhetoric of those who represent the dominant powers. The debate that should be taking place, in response to the liberal chaos, concerns the need for democratization and its relationship to social progress. Instead, we are given a lot of empty talk designed to evade the real problems: talk about 'good governance' (plus insipid flourishes about the 'struggle against corruption'!), which stands in for analysis of the real character of various regimes; talk in favour of communalist 'difference' and other postmodernist odds and ends; talk about an alleged clash of civilizations as a substitute for real debate about the clash of political cultures. We know how such discourse is relayed by the World Bank (the G7's propaganda ministry, as I call it) and foisted on the United Nations (which, I have to admit, puts up little resistance). As for the promised peace, it takes the form of permanent war (supposedly against 'terrorism'), repeated aggression by Washington and its allies ('preventive war'), and civil wars generated by the disintegration of states and societies that have followed the recipes of neoliberalism. The notion of a truncated democracy, which mainstream discourse presents together with the one-sided neoliberal doctrine of the supremacy of 'market laws', has been opening a rift between political rights (multiparty system, free and fair elections, etc.) and social rights. Far from addressing the real difficulties that need to be resolved, however gradually, or the complex interrelationship of the various dimensions of the demand for democracy, this simplistic answer merely sows confusion and encourages a number of dubious practices. Methodically applying the rule of double standards (military and other active support for the rights of one people, wilful blindness to those of another), the whole system threatens to lose its legitimacy in the eyes of growing numbers of individuals, movements and organizations, or even entire peoples.

In this framework, the dominant system endeavours to make international business law the supreme reference, taking precedence over national legislation in the spheres of commercial and labour law, company law, civil law and, of course, public and private international law. The World Trade Organization has accordingly drawn up a battery of principles and procedures, even going so far as to define a curious jurisdictional system (the Dispute Settlement Body) based on denial of the basic democratic principle of the separation of powers. The minority constituted by the business world thus sets itself up as the supreme master of the economic, social and political life of the entire planet, and proclaims itself at once the highest legislator, the supra-state executive and the only 'judge' of its own actions. We are back with the way in which Venice used to be run, by an administrative council of the wealthiest merchants.

At national level, these practices help to ruin the credibility and legitimacy of democracy. Once the law of the market is treated as an absolute rule, once international business law as we know it is given supremacy, it is impossible to combine this with the principles of democracy: we need only think of Argentina, the most dramatic example of the failure of such an association. There is a danger that such negative developments will lead to a strengthening of anti-democratic attitudes; these are already spreading like wildfire in both North and South, whether in the form of neopopulism (sometimes virtually equivalent to neofascism) or real or imaginary 'communal' identities (in the name of a chauvinist nationalism or 'religious specificities' prone to political manipulation).

At world level, the North's monopolistic position is being reinforced by the WTO and international business law (through the consolidation of intellectual and industrial property rights and commercial licences), and by the 'opening of capital accounts' (unrestricted international transfer, even of speculative capital). These reduce the hopes of so-called 'emergent' countries in their effort to catch up – which is based on the principles of competition in open markets – and increases the marginalization and exclusion of other regions (especially Africa) by sharpening the global polarization of wealth and power.

The crises that this unleashes have their roots in a quasi-libertarian belief that markets are the most advanced expression of liberty (understood as the liberty of 'individuals', abstracted from their inheritance and social environment), and that therefore all aspects of human and social life can and should be subordinate to the one-sided logic of the markets. The various models of a social contract and social security are then dismantled, for the sake of greater flexibility, and replaced with private contracts covering specific, exclusively defined groups. In many parts of civil society, this trend is felt to be inequitable and unacceptable. The dominant models do not allow for the slightest degree of state intervention, but on the contrary advocate an extreme concentration of power outside the control of parliament or citizens, in a multiplicity of supposedly 'technical' autonomous bodies (some of them private, despite the public character of their intervention). Similarly, a spirit of litigation in the sphere of social relations leads, in reality, to a growing delegation of power to 'judges'. Models of decentralization originally intended to bring power closer to the citizenry shape new centres where private interests rise free of all formal responsibility. The crisis-ridden political system thus becomes a patchwork quilt of interests, and the concern to devise coherent answers to problems is forgotten. This tendency strengthens the prejudice that 'there is no alternative'. The choices of a system of power that no longer has to give an account of itself thus become so many self-fulfilling prophecies. It is forgotten that the very definition of democracy entails the possibility of choosing between dIfferent alternatives.

Amid this general regression, the United Nations no longer has any particular functions to fulfil. It loses its two essential roles: to support democratization through the inclusion of social rights among the manifold rights of individuals and peoples; and to promote genuine international law, through the negotiation of step-by-step compromises indispensable to the progress of humanity.

The alternative: constructing social justice, international justice and a new popular sovereignty

Democracy is the product of modernity, defined as the conviction that human beings, individually and collectively, are alone responsible for shaping their future, and that there are always alternatives.

The real choice is therefore as follows: either we accept that socialization should take place solely in accordance with 'the market', at every level from the national to the global; or we seek to build (in the long term, by stages) the necessary forms for socialization through democracy, in the full, richest sense of the term. For the peoples of the world yearn simultaneously for social progress, democratic control of their lives, and respect for their national identity. And capitalism is less and less capable of allowing the real blossoming of these ideals, in individual countries or at the level of the world.

In destroying the basic values of universalism, the neoliberal slide illustrates the obsolescence of the capitalist mode. In its earlier stages, capitalism was universalist – even if the universalism was always truncated, because of the imperialist dimension inherent in its globalization. For its part, the alternative political culture of socialism is also universalist but, at the same time, potentially capable of going beyond the truncated universalism of capitalism. This culture of the future is not only a creative 'theoretical' utopia: it is already present in the consciousness of people living today. The true ideological/cultural conflict of the twenty-first century is not a Huntington-style 'clash of civilizations' but the clash between the political culture of capitalism (now drifting towards barbarism) and the political culture of socialism.

Faced with the boundless ambitions of the dominant forces in the world, it is necessary to oppose them with demands for a new law capable of ensuring that all the peoples of the world are treated with dignity, which is the prerequisite for their active and creative involvement in building the future. Proposals must also be made for a new juridical instrument sufficiently broad and multidimensional to take account of the rights of human beings (men and women, absolutely equal to one another), the rights of communities and peoples, and the right or legality governing relations among states.

The many complex issues that this raises may be summed up in one fundamental question: how should socialization operate? Purely through the constraints of 'the market', as deregulated as possible? Or through a combination of market and democracy? If the answer is the latter, the 'market' domain would have to be clearly identified and delimited; that is what is meant by 'social regulation of the market'. At the same time, democracy must be conceived in all its political, social and cultural dimensions, and, to support its practical deployment, it is necessary to think of ways of reforming existing institutions or creating new ones.

At the same time, the twofold principle of social and international justice must be affirmed as the core of any alternative model that is both legitimate and effective. This will mean formulating a set of precise proposals concerning positive rights, and establishing suitable institutional mechanisms to translate them into reality.

Social justice – to be achieved, initially, within the framework of national states – is the basis for any coherent programme to guarantee the rights of peoples. 'International justice' (or 'global justice') is the other dimension of a coherent programme to guarantee the rights of peoples. But we must recognize that respect for the sovereignty of nations and respect for human rights can sometimes enter into conflict with each other. Although the former should remain the cornerstone of international law, the sovereignty of states must be regarded as the sovereignty of the peoples concerned, not limited simply to their representation by the government authorities.

The following pages will present a programme of reforms for the institutional organization of globalization, consistent with the goal of multipolarity and capable of sustaining forms of democracy open to social progress. The programme concerns the United Nations. For the

UN must be the body within which international law is drafted: there is no more acceptable body for that purpose. Doubtless this implies reforms that will offer the ways and means (including institutional innovations) for real social forces to be present alongside the governments which, at best, represent them only imperfectly. It also implies that international laws, based on respect for sovereignty, will find their place in a coherent regulatory structure governing the rights of individuals and peoples, as well as the economic and social rights never mentioned in the neoliberal creed.

The conflict between sovereignty and democracy cannot be overcome through the 'right of interference' proposed by Western civil society, which, with characteristic naivety, makes itself a party to the manipulations of the dominant imperialist capital in pursuit of its own objectives. The kind of interference that is being talked about is nothing new: it has been the everyday practice of dominant capital for five centuries. Shrouded in a succession of legitimatory discourses (Christianization of 'the pagans', a civilizing colonial mission, now a 'crusade' for democracy), it has been experienced by its victims as the catastrophe of modern times up to and including genocide (a systematic practice among English settlers in North America, Australia, Tasmania and New Zealand, as among Argentineans and Chileans in Patagonia). Far from fostering the progress of other peoples, imperialist interference has always sought to strengthen the rule of reactionary local allies. It went through a period of retreat, between 1945 and 1980, and it was that retreat which made possible the limited advances of the peoples of Asia and Africa. A return to the principle of outside interference is not an advance in the universalization of democracy; it is a deviation from that cause. I therefore call for any such right to be condemned without reservation.

The conflict between sovereignty and democracy should be overcome by other means, which will require the mobilization of progressive forces within the societies concerned and support for them by the revived bodies of multipolar globalization (above all the UN system). Such active support may take various forms according to the gravity of the situation: from economic coercion to assistance and even arms supplies for insurgent forces (as in the case of the national liberation struggles). It is certainly a difficult road and success is never guaranteed. But there is no other.

The conditions must be created for the UN to fulfil its functions as the guardian of peace. The first of these conditions is disarmament: a multipolar world is a disarmed world. But we have to be clear that this means, first and foremost, disarmament of the most powerful – the United States, above all. Iraq was attacked not because it had weapons of mass destruction, but because it did not have them. The arrogance of the United States, which does not hide its readiness to use all weapons, even nuclear, if it considers them 'useful' (and on this point the US ruling class can 'convince' or manipulate its public without difficulty), actually serves to legitimize the arming of other countries under threat. The hypocrisy of the 'non-proliferation treaty' should therefore be exposed. The naive argument that poor countries could make better use of their resources feigns blindness to the real threat that imperialism poses to them. No doubt, when the dominant comprador classes purchase weapons from the United States, they do not do it to face down the imperialist enemy (which is actually their protector!); in fact, in the case of the Gulf oil states, such imports are scarcely more than a subsidy to the US Treasury. Nor can there be any doubt that the aim of disarmament should be to dismantle the networks that supply light weapons (and anti-personnel mines) and fuel the terrible civil wars accompanying the empire of chaos. But we should not allow the trees to obscure the forest: the North's permanent war against the South on which Washington and its allies have embarked. Removal of the US military bases covering the planet is a preliminary condition for general disarmament.

If a polycentric and pluralist model of globalization is to be re-built, offering a vision of progress to vulnerable regions that lack the means to take advantage of their insertion into global competition, then institution-building will have to take place at a regional as well as global level. For the multipolar world will have to involve a process of regionalization. This represents a challenge for all – the peoples of the European Union as well as eastern Europe, those of Asia as well as Africa and Latin America. The existing regional structures – NAFTA and MERCOSUR; the Cotonou accords between the ACP group of states and the EU, as well as the Regional Economic Partnership Accords (REPAs) due to succeed them; the Euromed project, ECWAS, COMESA and other regional African institutions, APEC – all these should be discussed with regard to the demands of international justice and a non-polarized model of globalization. To what extent are these existing regional models no more than transmission belts for neoliberal globalization? Under what conditions might they serve as building blocks for an alternative globalization?

The necessary transformations are such that regions cannot be merely economic groupings, especially of the neoliberal kind. They must also be conceived as political areas and define a social content capable of strengthening the position of the working classes and the underprivileged subregions.

The reform programme should therefore make it possible to combine respect for the sovereignty of peoples (gradually taking over from the sovereignty of states) with the democracy that is its precondition. This project for a humanist response to the challenge of globalization does not belong to the realm of utopia. On the contrary, it is the only possible realistic project, in the sense that the first advances towards it – coming in response to demands already powerfully formulated in contemporary societies – would everywhere win the support of strong social forces capable of driving them forward.

The proposed sovereignty of the peoples, based on the principles of democracy and social justice, requires mobilization of all the energies capable of creative imagination, and recognition of the diversity of their contributions. To be sure, cultural diversity is a fact of life, and it will remain so despite the advances of globalization. Democratic principle implies real respect for diversity (national, ethnic, religious, cultural or ideological) and tolerates no violation of this rule. Otherwise, diversity would inevitably become the plaything of opportunistic political forces, and indeed the present success of culturalism is due to the failures of an undemocratic management of diversity. Culturalism, for its part, claims that the differences in question are 'primordial' and based on unvarying historical characteristics, and that they should therefore have precedence over class differences, for example. This latter point is often found among religious forms of culturalism, which are in danger of sliding over into obscurantism and fanaticism.

Beyond diversity 'inherited from the past' – which should be recognized, and whose claims should be respected even though they are not adequate responses to today's problems – there is another, more interesting type of diversity that is turned towards the future and operates within a perspective of social transformation in response to today's challenges. This is the product of the diverse fundamental principles that underpin the various 'schools of social and economic ethics'. Genuine democracy and pluralism are based upon recognition of the diversity of alternatives that they imply.

Economic and social ethics provides the theoretical foundation for any coherent conception of a legitimate and equitable legal framework. This important theme in philosophical debates serves to identify the under-lying principles of the various schools of thought, such as utilitarianism, libertarianism (the inspiration for some of today's neoliberal practices), so-called 'egalitarian' liberalism à la Rawls, varieties of socialism or liberation theology. The analyses and proposals put forward in economics and political science are ultimately – if only implicitly – determined by the ethical principles to which we have been referring. A debate should therefore be launched on these fundamental issues, in order to build a convergence within diversity that is the only way of 'changing the world'.

Proposals for a renaissance of the UN

The following proposals are grouped into four sets, corresponding to the functions for which one would like to see the UN assume major responsibilities.

Proposals concerning the UN's political functions

The UN should be fully restored to its major responsibility of ensuring the security of peoples (and states), safeguarding the peace, prohibiting aggression on any pretext whatever (such as those mendaciously invoked on the occasion of the Iraq war). This principle should again be clearly proclaimed.

In this spirit, it is necessary to condemn unequivocally the statements whereby the US government, Nato and the G7 have assumed 'responsi-bilities' that are not theirs. Political plans should further be worked out to solve issues regarding the future of countries subjected to illegitimate intervention by the imperialist powers (former Yugoslavia, Afghanistan, Iraq). These plans should explicitly provide for the withdrawal of foreign military forces. It is quite unacceptable to introduce the UN 'by the back door' to legitimize situations created by unauthorized military intervention. In such cases, the UN should be asked only to 'facilitate' the withdrawal of the invaders.

To restore this major function of the UN may obviously entail reforms in its institutional architecture. But care must be taken here. Some 'criticisms' of the UN, and hasty proposals to correct it, have as their objective not to strengthen its role but to domesticate it on behalf of the imperialist triad. Others, seemingly more 'democratic' and 'realistic', threaten to be no more worthwhile. One thinks here, in particular, of the various attacks on veto rights: it is not hard to imagine that, if France had not been one of the beneficiaries, the United States would not have succeeded in legitimizing its aggression in Iraq. Before any reform of the Security Council is proposed (enlargement to include India and Brazil or to ensure greater representation of various regions in the world), it should be subject to careful consideration; it might be that the main issue then would be to give the General Assembly greater importance and to make its resolutions – whether or not they have the force of law, in precisely defined hypothetical situations – more geared to the actions required of the Security Council.

To restore this central function of the UN does not imply a return to the 'absolute' sovereignty of states, considered as sole representatives of their peoples. But it does imply absolute respect for the sovereignty of peoples.

Restoration of the UN's functions should permit effective progress towards a solution of the main crises of our time, which are largely produced (or intensified) by the strategies for the 'generalization of chaos' that certain powers, especially the United States, have brought into play. In this spirit, there should be action (i) to deploy a UN force between Israel (in its pre-1967 green line 'frontiers') and Palestine, it being understood that Israel would not be able to resist economic sanctions as severe as those imposed on other states; and (ii) to deploy UN peacekeeping forces in countries of the former Yugoslavia (Bosnia and Kosovo), and in African countries that have been the victim of so-called 'civil wars'. Such operations may be planned in close relationship with any regional organizations concerned (the European Union, wider Europe, the African Union).

The UN should actively participate in drafting a plan for general disarmament. This should not merely involve implementation of the non-proliferation treaty, which, in its present form, strengthens the monopoly of weapons of mass destruction enjoyed by those who have proved to be the most frequent uses of such weapons. Disarmament should begin with the major powers and be monitored by the UN, instead of being subject to the (now defunct) 'bipolar' control formerly exercised by the two superpowers. General disarmament should involve the removal of all military bases established by a state outside its national frontiers, and hence, most particularly, those through which the United States intends to exercise 'military control of the planet'.

The UN should participate in defining the framework, and the operational forms, for any 'humanitarian interventions'. The need for such interventions is not in doubt, given that, at the present stage of development, societies may suddenly sink into savagery (ethnocide, ethnic or religious cleansing, apartheid). But the responsibility for action cannot be left to the imperialist powers, since that would leave the field open to manipulation, 'double standards', and so on.

Similarly, the UN should bear the main collective responsibility for the definition of what constitute 'acts of terrorism'. It should also decide the conditions for, and monitor the implementation of, any operation to eradicate terrorist practices. The 'war on terrorism' cannot be entrusted to the great powers, and especially not to the United States.

Proposals concerning the rights of peoples and the drafting of international law

Our guiding principle here starts from the previous observation that the concept of state sovereignty needs to be redefined. Under certain conditions, respect for the principle of sovereignty and for the requirements of democracy may conflict with each other. But this contradiction cannot be resolved by abolishing one or other of its terms: the right of peoples (by keeping the old concept of sovereignty) or sovereignty itself (by justifying intervention and manipulation by the imperialist powers). The contradiction can be overcome only through real progress in the democratization of all societies. Admittedly this is a process that can only proceed at its own pace, in line with progress in affirmation of the need for democracy. The international organization should intervene here to support such progress, and to accelerate its expression in real changes to the way in which power is exercised. The United Nations, more than anywhere else, is the place where debate should be tirelessly pursued.

A set of declarations, covenants and conventions on human rights began a whole process of expanding how they are defined. The Universal Declaration of Human Rights (1948) was later supplemented by two covenants – the Covenant on Economic, Social and Cultural Rights and the Covenant on Civil and Political Rights, both adopted in Tehran in 1968 – which, taken together, clearly confirmed the move from a restricted conception of human rights (involving only civil and political rights) to a broader vision encompassing social and collective rights. In 1986 the UN General Assembly underlined this tendency with its Declaration on the Right to Development, which became an integral part of the corpus of human rights. Nevertheless, the effort must never be allowed to flag: the existing texts are still insufficient and, above all, are constantly challenged and ignored in practice – or else they are said to be inapplicable, especially when their economic, social and collective aspects conflict with the perceived interests of the triad powers. The rights of peoples to development, which have been deeply researched by 'private' circles such as the Lelio Basso Foundation and strongly promoted by partly state-based groupings such as the Non-Aligned Movement, are in practice largely denied to be universal rights taking precedence for individuals and peoples. Similarly, access to land for all peasants on earth (half of humanity) – as well as its logical concomitant: human and viable conditions for the working of the land – are rights that up to now have not even begun to be recognized.

It is within the same universal framework, represented by the United Nations, that efforts should continue to define rights that still command only embryonic, or anyway incomplete, recognition. Rights affirming the equality of men and women in principle, and looking towards their actual equality in practice, belong to the same family. The 'collective' rights through which cultural, linguistic, religious or other 'identities' are expressed must also be the object of profound discussion, with the aim of defining both the rights themselves and their fields of application. In no case should recognition of these rights to diversity permit demands for the 'communal organization' of society, which would negate the 'right to resemblance' and the rights of individuals outside their community. In other words, the rights in question cannot be invoked to challenge the principle of secularism.

Many 'realists' attach little importance to charters of rights, considering that they matter only in so far as measures are taken to ensure their practical effect. But this is probably to underestimate the importance of law, which can become an effective weapon if it is used to enforce respect. As we shall see, one way of upholding the operation of the law is to create a system of universal courts.

The UN should have particular responsibility in the drafting of international business law. The deepening of all manner of global economic relations makes it more necessary than ever to work out a system of international business law. This particular field of law must not, however, take precedence over the basic rights of individuals and peoples or over national formulations of those rights. In this respect, the course chosen for the draft Multilateral Agreement on Investment is unacceptable.

Furthermore, the task of drafting international business law cannot simply be entrusted to the partner represented by the collectivity of dominant capitalist interests (the 'Club of Transnationals'), as is the case in the WTO's projects, especially as the partner in question sets itself up as legislator, judge and interested party in sole control of its projected business tribunal. Rarely has anyone trampled with such impertinence on the elementary principles of legality and justice. If nothing comes of that, it would be no more acceptable that the courts of the United States (whose impartiality is more than doubtful) and the especially primitive laws of that country should govern the practical regulation of business affairs – although that is indeed increasingly the case today. International business law should be drafted through open debate among all the interested parties: not only the business world but also the state and the workers who will have to bear the consequences (both in the relevant companies and at the level of entire nations). There is no other forum for this debate than the UN (and the ILO, which is one of its expressions).

The UN cannot be erected overnight into a 'world state' or 'world government', nor even into a supranational authority with overarching powers in various areas, although this does not rule out the long-term possibility that it might move in that direction. In any event, proposals along these lines must be treated with great caution. Today we see a flurry of proposals claiming to associate 'civil society' (defined in the usual Washington style) with the life of the organization, and some of these proposals would like to give representation of 'the business world' a central place. By contrast, advocates of this kind of 'reform' of the UN always disregard the world of labour, the majority of human beings facing a tiny minority of billionaires, and have even gone so far as to seek reductions in the rather toothless powers of the ILO. Unfortunately, the ILO administration seems to be playing along with this plan to turn the social clock back.

Proposals for a 'world parliament', consisting of representatives of national parliaments (which in some cases do not even exist and are seldom truly representative of their peoples), are not necessarily anodyne or unrealistic. Moves in that direction could be started, even if we know that the democracy it is supposed to uphold cannot advance on a world scale more rapidly than at the level of the nations concerned.

Proposals concerning the economic management of globalization

The 'deregulated' globalization we see today – actually a globalization totally regulated by dominant capital and the G7 group of states politically beholden to it – is only one among several possible forms. It is neither 'inescapable' nor 'without an alternative' nor even acceptable; it is necessary to replace the existing institutional forms of world regulation, by supporting and perhaps supplementing the forms of national and regional regulation that the world's peoples establish here or there, and by accepting that in the modern world there may even be a contradiction or conflict between these different levels of economic management.

The task ahead is therefore complicated, and even if the UN mobilizes in support of it any progress will remain modest for a long time to come. But the advances that are made should not be treated lightly, as they point in directions favourable to the world's peoples and working classes.

In view of their hugely destructive effects, international debts might be a solid starting point for debate on the UN's functions in managing the world economy. Conventional discourse places all responsibility for the debt on the borrower countries, pointing to their unjustifiable record on corruption, the incompetence and irrationality of their political decision-makers, their extreme nationalism, and so forth. The reality is quite different. A large proportion of the loans were the result of systematic policies on the part of lenders seeking to invest surplus capital – capital which, owing to the economic crisis of the last twenty years, found no outlet in productive investment, either in the rich countries or in those ostensibly capable of handling it. Alternative outlets were therefore artificially fabricated to avoid the devalorization of this surplus capital. The explosive boom in speculative movements of very short-term investment capital is the result of these policies, as is their investment in the debt of third world countries and the former Eastern bloc. No allusion is ever made to the major share of responsibility borne by the World Bank, in particular, but also by the transnationals and many of the large private banks in the USA, Europe and Japan. 'Corruption' was an additional aspect in these policies, with the complicity of the lenders (World Bank, private banks, TNCs) and state officials concerned with countries in the South and East. A systematic 'audit' of international debts should therefore be an immediate priority. It would show that much of the debt in question is juridically illegitimate.

The weight of debt service is strictly unbearable, not only for the poorest countries but also for others in the South. We should recall here that after the First World War, when Germany was ordered to pay reparations to the value of 7 per cent of its exports, liberal economists of the day concluded that it was an intolerable burden to which Germany's productive apparatus would be unable to adjust. Yet today, economists belonging to the same liberal school have no qualms about proposing the 'adjustment' of third world economies to levels of debt service five to ten times higher. In reality, then, debt service is today a way of pillaging the wealth and labour of the peoples of the South (and East), an especially lucrative way because it has even turned the poorest countries on earth into exporters of capital to the North. It is also a particularly brutal form, which releases dominant capital from worries and uncertainties about the management of companies and hired workforces. The debt service falls due – that's all they need to know. It is up to the states concerned (not to the capitalist lenders) to extract it from the labour of their peoples.

A 'classification' of international debts is the next priority. They may be grouped under the following three categories.

- *Odious and immoral debts* A fine example of these is the government loans contracted by apartheid South Africa, which were used to buy weapons to crush the revolt of its African people.
- *Dubious debts* These are mostly the result of loans suggested by the financial powers of the North (including the World Bank), involving corrupt procedures in which the creditors were as much actors as the debtors. In the majority of cases, where, as the lenders knew, the money was not even invested in the projects that served as cover, the debts are purely and simply illegal in the eyes of any justice worthy of the name. In a few cases the loans actually were invested, but in absurd projects imposed by the lenders (especially the World Bank) – so, once again, it is the Bank that should be on trial. But that institution is not financially 'responsible', as it places itself above the law and the liberal discourse of 'risk'.
- *Acceptable debts* When loans really were used for the intended purposes, there is no doubt that they should be recognized.

Not only odious and immoral debts should be unilaterally repudiated (after due audit); the same applies to payments already made to service them, which creditors should reimburse after capitalization at the same rates of interest that the debtors had to bear. It would then be clear that, in fact, it is the North which is in debt to the South. The kind of debt management on offer to the 'highly indebted poor countries' (HIPCs) obeys a quite different logic. The whole debt is treated as perfectly legitimate, without any examination or audit, and any forgiveness proposal is presented as a simple question of charity. The stated aim is to 'relieve the burden' for the very poor countries, but at the same time to impose on them further draconian conditions that would make them akin to colonies under direct foreign administration.

Apart from an audit and measures to discharge the debt, it is necessary to ensure that similar situations do not arise in the future, by expanding the still rudimentary international law on debt and setting up real courts to hand down rulings. This would take things much further than one can expect from any arbitration commissions.

To give the UN back all its responsibility for organization of the world economic system means to redefine the functions of the major institutions within its ambit (UNCTAD and the ILO among others) or outside it (WTO, IMF and World Bank). The main priorities in this field might be the following:

- To breathe new life into UNCTAD and give it new (or revived) functions, such as the drafting of a foreign investment code to regulate relocation and protect the workforce of all the parties concerned, and the negotiation of market access for the various national and regional partners. These tasks would challenge the complete marginalization to which UNCTAD is presently subject; the organization needs to be thoroughly overhauled if it is to break out of an orbit rigidly defined by the Club of the Transnationals.
- To breathe new life into the ILO, not in the sense proposed by its present leadership but, on the contrary, in a way that strengthens workforce representation and workers' rights.
- To renegotiate the global monetary system and the institutionalized regional arrangements to stabilize exchange rates, in such a way that a new IMF, having little in common with the present organization, would have responsibility for managing the linkage between the various regional systems. As things stand today, the IMF – which is not responsible for the relationship among the main currencies (dollar, yen, pound sterling, Swiss franc) – operates as a collective colonial monetary authority on behalf of the triad, whose task it is to manage the finances of dependent countries by imposing 'structural adjustment' and subjecting them to resource pillage for the benefit of footloose capital and tribute-like debt service.
- To construct a global capital market worthy of the name, which steers capital into productive investment (in both the North and the South) and, as a necessary complement, has the tools to discourage 'speculative' finance flows. (The Tobin tax could be one idea in this context.) Such a development would place a question mark over the functions of the World Bank and the World Trade Organization.

Of course, in the field of economic management, the UN cannot do more than it is able to do in global political management. But it can begin the process of building global economic government and a global economic policy. And, in saying government, one is saying finances in the same breath.

The management of natural resources is undoubtedly the best first approach. Today, access to natural resources is in principle still an issue of national sovereignty, but this has often been flouted by colonial situations (where all sovereignty disappears) and what are commonly known as 'geopolitical' relationships of forces. In fact, unequal access to natural resources is at the root of the huge waste perpetrated by the societies of the North, on a planet where it is impossible to imagine a generalization of the North's modes of consumption, and where the established form of globalization therefore condemns the rest of the world's peoples to the status of victims of 'global apartheid'. The ecological movements, which first raised levels of awareness of this dramatic problem, have not really persuaded the intergovernmental system (represented by the Rio and Kyoto conferences and the Johannesburg follow-up in August 2002) to accept adequate and effective forms of global democratic management of resource access. The militarization of globalization should also be related to the aim of the hegemonic power to control the world's natural resources.

Exploitation of these resources is in principle a matter for 'actually existing capitalism', which is based on short-term calculation of financial profitability; the transnational corporations that take the decisions are not even aware that other calculations are a possibility. This is truly an area where the supposed rationality of the market is in fact irrational from the point of view of the long-term interests of the peoples concerned. The idea of 'sustainable development' stems from a new awareness of this contradiction between the market and the interests of humanity, but those who argue for the idea often do not spell out its practical consequences.

The alternative of rational ('sustainable') democratic management of natural resources (at both local and global levels) could be discussed on the basis of certain proposals that are beginning to emerge: for a global tax on profits associated with access to, and exploitation of, natural resources, or for distribution of this tax revenue in ways that benefit the peoples concerned, by encouraging the development of poorer countries and regions and discouraging waste. This could lead to the rudiments of a system of global taxation. It would cover a large number of natural resources – from oil and minerals to water and climate. But the suggestion is that the debate should start on oil and water.

The UN should oversee management of water, as a common good of humanity. There can be no life without water, which is as necessary as the air we breathe. Of the many uses of water, we shall here focus only on those related to agriculture, which consumes the greatest share.

For natural reasons, the distribution of water among the various rural societies on earth is extremely uneven. Some regions receive water free, from the heavens, while people in arid or semi-arid zones have to search for it in rivers or deep wells, and then spread it through irrigation to all the agricultural land. In the latter case, the production costs of water are a long way from zero. Should the scarcity therefore be reflected in the attachment of a price to water resources?

By shutting oneself up in conventional economic thinking and the market alienation on which it is based, by playing the game of competitiveness in a context of unbridled globalization, one accepts that the remuneration of labour will be lower for some than for others – unless, that is, one decides this it is not worth continuing to produce at all. Neoliberal globalization condemns agriculture to disappear from huge regions of the planet.

It is a fact that peoples, nations and states exist: they occupy different spaces on earth and do not enjoy the same natural conditions. A realistic political economy must take account of this. Conventional economics, which pretends to ignore these dimensions of reality, substitutes the theory of an imaginary globalized world, defined by worldwide commodification of all aspects of social life and all conditions surrounding human activity. This enables it to legitimize the one-sided thrust of capital. If liberal economists, who defend this capitalist fundamentalism, were consistent with themselves, they would conclude that the optimum use of natural resources (in this case, water) requires huge resettlement of the world population in accordance with the uneven distribution of resources on the surface of the globe. Water would then become a common good of the whole of humanity.

Meanwhile, water is among the common goods of this or that people or country: if it is relatively scarce, access to it has to be rationalized; the cost of its use must be shared among all the inhabitants of the country in one way or another – that is, through market regulation or an acceptable system of taxes and subsidies. The formula used in working out that system will involve a set of compromises defined by internal social conditions and the country's precise insertion into the world economy: compromises between the peasantry and consumers of food products; compromises between the social project of economic development and the export levels required at a given stage of that project (perhaps involving subsidization of 'naturally' uncompetitive exports). The precise formula cannot, however, be laid down once and for all; it will always be relative and temporally specific.

The answer to these problems lies in the field of what we should call 'the legal rights of peoples and humanity'. So far as water is concerned, such rights are still virtually non-existent, since each country is in principle free to use as it sees fit any underground or surface water within its own frontiers, and if an agreement exists at all it is simply the consequence of a broader international treaty. It has now become an urgent matter for the world's peoples, for humanity as a whole, to acquire genuine legal rights on this issue. International business law, dictated by the interests of capital and currently formulated entirely by special international institutions (mainly the WTO), is no substitute – quite the contrary – for the missing right of peoples to manage water resources as a common human good.

Proposals concerning the institutionalization of international justice

Several international courts of justice already exist: some even predate the creation of the United Nations, while others are a more recent result of the denunciation of war crimes and crimes against humanity. Yet this archipelago of international justice remains largely ineffectual, both because of the restrictive definition of its powers and because certain countries (the United States, in particular) refuse to accept its legitimacy. The first task here must be to draw up a full inventory of existing fixtures, to analyse the inadequacies of the relevant institutions, and to focus on the legal vacuums that one would like to see gradually filled.

There are also a number of so-called 'public opinion tribunals' (the Bertrand Russell War Crimes Tribunal is a fine example), which do not enjoy legal status yet fulfil highly useful functions in alerting the public. Their mission deserves to continue, with an even greater sphere of activity and international resonance. But this should not stand in the way of campaigns to set up recognized international courts that have the power to hand down legal judgements, nor of action to codify laws that the courts in question will be charged to uphold.

Work must also be done on designing an international court of justice to complement and crown the proposals in previous sections concerning the responsibilities of the UN. Three sets of courts seem particularly desirable in this connection.

The first group of juridical institutions concerns the political aspects of managing globalization. Although a state's action or intervention outside its frontiers, on whatever grounds, should always be submitted for the judgement of the United Nations, it is advisable that a juridical institution coming under the UN should have a say on whether such intervention should be authorized or condemned. The International Court of Justice in the Hague certainly has the competence, but under present conditions lacks the appropriate powers of execution. For example, when Sandinista Nicaragua registered a complaint over the US Navy's mining of its ports, the Court found in favour of the plaintiff and demanded that the guilty party cease its armed interference and pay damages to the victim, yet the judgement remained a dead letter as only the UN Security Council, where the United States has veto rights, could provide for its enforcement. On 27 June 1986 the Court ordered the United States to pay reparations of $17 billion, but Nicaragua never received a single cent. Similarly, the Court's recent judgement on the 'wall of shame' in occupied Palestine – the grounds for which are quite unambiguous – could be followed through only with a non-binding 'recommendation' by the UN General Assembly. A review is therefore necessary to enlarge the powers of the Court. One can imagine that the state which is the aggrieved party, or else the UN General Assembly, might not only have recourse to the Court but also have an assurance that a judgement in its favour will actually take effect, even if this is resisted by the state responsible for the illegal act of intervention. Unless this happens, the imperialist powers (especially the United States) can never be judged for the most naked violations of international law, or, if they are, will be liable only to sanctions that popular mobilizations can impose on them.

A second group of juridical institutions is needed to consolidate the rights of individuals and peoples recognized by the UN. One inspiration here might be the European Court of Justice, which, on matters within its competence, may be directly approached by aggrieved parties (individuals or collectives), without the need for prior official authorization in the country to which they belong. But another possibility would – indeed should – be to enlarge the domain of international justice to include social and other rights, perhaps with separate chambers of the UN's court handling the rights of individuals and peoples.

A third group of juridical institutions should be created to deal with business law. Here again one might imagine separate chambers of the UN's Business Court, each with specific competences, one of which would have the task of judging criminal economic acts. The case of Bhopal illustrates the scandalous impunity that the transnational corporations enjoy at the present time.

It would also be in this framework that another chamber of the Court might deal with disputes concerning external debts.

A plan for action

The above proposals are certainly ambitious, and their implementation even in part will require considerable time. But the future begins today, and there is no reason to put off launching a plan of action to ensure that progress is made.

It does not seem useful to call on governments today to start negotiating on a 'reform of the UN'. They will do it themselves if they deem it necessary. But the current relationship of forces is such that any reforms, if put into practice, are unlikely to lead in the right direction. On the contrary, there is every reason to believe that they will fit into the dominant imperialist strategies of the hour, which seek to marginalize and domesticate still further the international organization. It seems more likely that there will be a need to campaign against such reforms rather than in their favour.

In my view, then, a different approach is necessary – one that directly addresses public opinion. I would propose establishing a number of ad hoc international commissions (on each of the themes of the project we have outlined), which might then supply with analysis and further proposals the huge cluster of movements that recognize themselves in the national, regional and world forums. The World Forum for Alternatives, through the centres of critical thought constituted by its network of correspondents and associates, might help to coordinate the enterprise.

Once the work of the commissions was sufficiently advanced, it could – and should – become the focus of worldwide campaigns on a number of clearly defined objectives for each issue. This would help to correct the imbalances that mark the typical relationship of forces in the contemporary world.

CHAPTER 7

Conclusions

The difficulties of constructing a multipolar world

The challenges to the construction of a genuinely multipolar world are more serious than many 'alter-globalization' movements imagine. They are also plural in nature, and this is reflected in the title of this concluding chapter.

First of all, we have to classify the difficulties, to identify those which could (or should) be overcome in the initial phase (the 'short term') and those which can be overcome only gradually in the course of decades. These challenges take on their full meaning only if we situate them within 'the long transition beyond capitalism' (or, to put it less indirectly, 'the long transition to world socialism'). At the same time, we have to assess the scale of the challenges in question, which are not the same from one country or region to another. The existing governments (or those likely to take over from them in the foreseeable future) have their own views of the challenges they think they are facing, which are not necessarily those that seem to us the 'real' challenges for our project of building a genuinely multipolar world. Nevertheless, we cannot simply dismiss with contempt the views of existing governments, if only because they inspire the actions they take today or will take in the period ahead. The protest movements themselves do not always share the same idea of the challenges. Nor can we ignore the diverse, or even conflicting, character of their analyses of 'reality', or of their projects for society.

What I wanted to stress in this work requires an explicit identification of the short-term and longer-term challenges. The main immediate task is to frustrate Washington in its military project: this is the absolute prerequisite for creating the leeway we need, and without it any social or democratic progress and any advance towards a multipolar world will remain vulnerable in the extreme. In the face of this challenge, then, 'politics' in the current sense of the term, and therefore the role of state policies and decisions, will still be decisive.

The overweening character of the US project means that it is bound to fail in the end, though at a terrible human cost. The resistance of its victims – the peoples of the South – will grow stronger as the Americans become bogged down in the many war fronts to which they are forced to commit themselves. The resistance will eventually defeat the enemy, and perhaps also awaken public opinion in the United States, as it did in the case of the Vietnam War. But it would be much better to halt the catastrophe sooner – which international diplomacy could succeed in doing, especially if Europe measured up to its responsibilities.

In the longer term, a 'different globalization' will involve challenging the options of neoliberal capitalism and the way in which collective triad imperialism runs the affairs of the planet within the framework of an extreme, or more 'balanced', Atlanticism. Since the building of the future always begins today, it is necessary to embark on this road without waiting any longer. As I see things, the short-term task (frustrating the American project) and the long-term task (building a multipolar world) do not refer to consecutive objectives; the tasks overlap with each other. Besides, the peoples of the world do not wait before taking action on social and democratic issues, whenever they consider that their interests are threatened or that they are in a position to make a breakthrough. There is absolutely no reason to call for such struggles to be given up while we wait for the defeat of the United States. On the contrary, social or democratic advances here and now help to put Washington's project to flight.

Progress along these lines will certainly not be so swift as to make unnecessary a number of (initially modest) intermediate objectives. But the insertion of these into a long-term perspective is the only way of ensuring that they will be effective. So far as I am concerned, that long-term perspective is one of a long transition to world socialism, for only then can the goal of a genuinely multipolar world be attained.

In fact, the multipolar world is not 'the end of history' – which for me is a non-concept. It will be a gradual process of construction, never complete, always evolving. In the foreseeable or even distant future, neither the social systems of the different partners (all the countries in the world) nor the equilibrium (or disequilibrium) characterizing their insertion into globalization will come to the end of their evolution (if that means anything, which I doubt).

Can Washington's military project be thwarted?

Concerning the first priority objective – to thwart Washington's military project – the analyses in previous chapters underline the many difficult obstacles that have to be overcome.

The present moment is characterized by the deployment of a North American project for world hegemony, the only one that today occupies the whole stage. There is no longer any counter-project to limit the area under US control, as there used to be in the era of bipolarism (1945–90). The European project, apart from its inherent ambiguities, has gone into a period of withdrawal. The countries of the South (the Group of 77, the Non-Aligned Movement), which in the Bandung era (1955–75) aimed to oppose a common front to Western imperialism, have given up the project. China itself, going it alone, seeks little more than to protect its (anyway ambiguous) national project, and does not present itself as an active partner in the reshaping of the world.

The 'European project' is not going in the direction that is needed to bring Washington to its senses. Indeed, it remains a basically 'non-European' project, scarcely more than the European part of the American project. The EU's planned constitution is for a Europe that is settling into its dual neoliberal and Atlanticist option. Hence the potential contained in the clash of political cultures, which could theoretically lead to an end of Atlanticism, remains mortgaged to the social-liberalism of the majority sections of the left (electorally speaking, the European socialist parties). But social-liberalism is a contradiction in terms, since liberalism is by nature non-social, or even anti-social.

Russia, China and India are the three strategic opponents of Washington's project, and the existing governments in these countries are probably increasingly aware of it. But they appear to believe that they can manoeuvre and avoid directly clashing with the US administration, or even that they can use the 'friendship' of the United States in the conflicts that oppose them to one another (Russia's fears of Chinese expansion in Siberia, the India–China conflict). The 'common front against terrorism', to which they appear to subscribe, has somewhat confused the issue. But here we see Washington's double game at work: on the one hand, the USA supports the Chechens, Uighurs and Tibetans (as it has the Islamist movements in Algeria, Egypt and elsewhere); on the other hand, it waves the fight against Islamic terrorism as a flag to rally Moscow, Beijing and Delhi. So far, at least, it is a game that seems to have worked.

A Eurasian rapprochement (Europe + Russia + China + India), which would certainly carry with it the rest of Asia and Africa and isolate the United States, is certainly desirable. There are even a few signs pointing in that direction. But we are a long way from seeing its crystallization put an end to Europe's Atlanticist option.

'World history' was for long a history of complementarity and conflict among the major societies of the 'Old World' (Asia, Europe, Africa), with the post-Columbian Americas as the stage for the 'isolationist' expansion of the main power constituted there, the United States. Since 1945 that power has asserted its global calling, initially under a compulsion to share it unevenly with its Soviet military and ideological rival, but without an apparent equal following the collapse of 'socialism'. Faced with this American challenge, could the centres of the Old World impose a new equilibrium by drawing closer together?

The analyses in this book suggest a very cautious answer. The work of construction remains fragile in two major partners of the system (China and a Europe mired in Atlanticism), while Japan, India and Russia are no less vulnerable. Nevertheless, the American project of sole world leadership will not necessarily win through. The forging of political alliances among the main European states, Russia and Asia (especially China and India) is now on the agenda, and if it happens it will finally put paid to Washington's inordinate designs. Multipolarity will then provide the framework for the possible and necessary overcoming of capitalism. The stable and genuinely multipolar world will be socialist or it will not exist at all.

My earlier remarks concerning Japan and the United States indicate two further obstacles to be overcome if Washington's project is to be defeated. For there is very little sign of an awakening of the Japanese people, and still less of the American people.

Can the countries of the South play an active role in seeing off the US military projects? The peoples under attack certainly can, and for the moment they are the only active opponents of those projects. However – at least partly because they are alone and feel it – the methods of their just struggle are of questionable effectiveness and involve instruments that delay the crystallization of solidarity among the peoples of the North. On the other hand, my analysis of the 'compradorization' of ruling classes and regimes throughout the South suggests that, for all their evident 'fundamentalism' (Islamist, Hindu or ethnicist), not much can be expected of the governments currently in office there, or likely to take over soon. To be sure, they are shaken by Washington's boundless arrogance and worried about the hostility (not to say hatred) that their peoples display towards the United States. But are they capable of doing anything other than accept what fate has in store for them?

In fact, the South in general no longer has a project of its own, as it used to have in the Bandung era. No doubt the ruling classes of the so-called 'emergent' countries (China, Korea, Southeast Asia, India, Brazil and a few others) are pursuing goals that they seem to define themselves, and for the attainment of which their respective states are actively working. These goals may be summed up in a single formula: growth maximization within the system of globalization. The countries in question dispose – or think they dispose – of enough bargaining power to derive greater profit from their 'selfish' strategy than from an airy 'common front' with others weaker than themselves. But the advantages are specific to the particular fields of interest to them; they do not call into question the general architecture of the system. Indeed, they do not give to the vague (illusory) project of building a 'national capitalism' the degree of coherence that would define a truly alternative project for society. The most vulnerable countries of the South (the 'fourth world') do not even have a project they can call their own; religious or ethnicist fundamentalism does not qualify to be described as one, being more in the nature of a makeshift substitute. As we have seen, the North takes the initiative of advancing its own projects 'for them' (we should rather say:

against them) – as in the case of the EU–ACP association (the 'economic partnership agreements' scheduled to replace the Cotonou accords) or the 'Euro-Mediterranean dialogue', or the US–Israeli plans for the Middle East or even the 'Greater Middle East'.

Thinking long-term

The perspectives change when they are placed in a longer-term framework. For, contrary to the dictum of egoistic pragmatism, the deluge will not come *après moi*. It is the task of grand politics to think of the long-term, and here the key role of possible changes in the social, national and international relationship of forces comes into its own.

There are no 'laws of capitalist expansion' that assert themselves as a quasi-supernatural force. There is no historical determinism prior to history itself. Tendencies inherent in the logic of capital encounter the resistance of forces that do not accept its effects. Real history is therefore the outcome of this conflict between the logic of capitalist expansion and other logics stemming from the resistance of social forces that suffer the effects of such expansion.

For example, the industrialization of the periphery in the 1945–90 period was not the natural result of capitalist expansion; rather, the national liberation victories imposed industrialization and global capital had to adjust to it. Again, the declining efficacy of the national state, produced by capitalist globalization, is not an irreversible determinant of the future; national reactions may indeed set the process of globalization on an unexpected course – for better or for worse, according to the circumstances. Or again, environmental concerns that conflict with the essentially short-term logic of capital might eventually force important changes in the direction of capitalist adjustment. The list of examples could go on and on.

An effective response to these challenges can be found only if we understand that history is governed not by the unfailing deployment of pure economic laws but by social reactions to the tendencies expressed in them – reactions which, in turn, define the social relations in the framework of which those laws operate. 'Anti-systemic forces' – if this is how we should call the organized, consistent and effective refusal to bow unilaterally to these supposed laws (actually, just the law of profit peculiar to capitalism) – shape real history as much as does any pure logic of capitalist accumulation. They dictate the possibilities and forms of expansion, which then takes place within the organized framework that the forces of resistance have imposed.

The method advocated here rules out advance 'recipes' for the shaping of the future. The future is produced through changes in the social and political relationship of forces, themselves produced through struggles whose outcome is not known in advance. We may nevertheless reflect on the future, with a view to helping the crystallization of coherent and feasible projects and assisting society to overcome the false solutions that threaten to drag it into the mire.

As we argued in the last chapter, the project of a humanist response to the challenge of globalized expansion is not at all 'utopian'; on the contrary, it is the only realistic project. To identify the conditions for such a response to be effective, we must start from the diversity of the motives that determine popular mobilization and social struggles. The various aspirations that serve as motives may perhaps be grouped under five headings: (i) political democracy and respect for the law and intellectual freedom; (ii) social justice; (iii) respect for different groups and communities; (iv) better ecological management; (v) a more favourable position within the world system.

It is easy to see that the movement activists corresponding to these different aspirations are rarely the same. For example, a concern to give one's country a higher place in the world hierarchy, defined in terms of wealth, power and scope for initiative, may strike a chord among the whole population, but it will probably be uppermost in the minds of the ruling classes and state officials. The yearning for respect – in the full sense of really equal treatment – may mobilize women as a group, or a cultural, linguistic or religious group that is subject to discrimination; the movements inspired by it may therefore embrace more than one class. By contrast, the yearning for greater social justice, defined as greater material welfare, more pertinent and effective legislation or a radically different system of social and productive relations, will almost inevitably become inserted into the class struggle: for example, into demands by all or part of the peasantry for land reform, redistribution of property, protenant legislation, more favourable prices, and so on; or into demands for trade-union rights, labour legislation or even a policy of more effective government intervention, including forms of nationalization, workers' participation, and so on. But it is also possible, for instance, that various professions or employers' groups will demand an easing of the tax burden. And social movements may address their message to the whole population, by demanding proper education, health care and housing as universal rights, or more suitable ways of caring for the environment. Democratic aspirations may be limited and precise, especially when they inspire a movement in opposition to an undemocratic regime, but they may also be more broadly conceived as a lever to promote the full range of social demands.

A current map of these movements would undoubtedly show huge unevenness in their distribution on the ground. As we know, however, the map is shifting, since wherever a problem arises there is potentially nearly always a movement to find a solution. But one would have to be naively optimistic to imagine that the sum of forces operating in the most diverse terrains will yield a coherent movement of the whole society for greater justice and democracy. Chaos is as much part of nature as order. Similar naivety would be required to discount the likely reactions of governments to these movements. Geopolitics and governments' strategies to deal with the national and international challenges facing them correspond to other logics than those underlying the aspirations in question.

The critique I would make of Hardt and Negri fits in with these reflections. For, in their book *Empire*, they continue on a path first opened by Manuel Castells in *The Rise of the Network Society*, failing to see that the 'networks' they hail as alternatives are limited to a few segments of triad societies and are always subject to the dominant capitalist logic. The woolly concept of 'multitudes', with no frontiers and no structures, also chimes with the banal old discourse of North American political liberalism; it is little more than a synonym for the non-concept 'the people', which derives from a vision of society reduced to the sum of its individuals. It should be the source of severe and unbending criticism that such nonsense receives the accolades of large parts of 'civil society' (another woolly concept, almost a non-concept), and that the work of Hardt and Negri is arrogantly presented as a 'manifesto of alter-globalization'. The 'movement' will advance only if it shakes off such illusions, which at best are proof of astonishing naivety.

This tells us that manipulation or instrumentalization of social movements is always a possibility capable of condemning them to impotence, or of forcing them to fit into a perspective that was not theirs to begin with. There is a global political strategy for running the world, whose aim is to fragment anti-systemic forces by encouraging the break-up of state forms of social organization. As many Slovenias, Chechnyas, Kosovos and Kuwaits as possible! Identity demands, or anyway the possibility of their manipulation, are a welcome godsend in this connection. This makes the question of identity – communal, ethnic, religious or other – one of the central issues of our time.

The basic democratic principle that involves real respect for national, ethnic, religious, cultural and ideological diversity must not be violated. Diversity cannot be handled in any other way than through the sincere practice of democracy – otherwise, it inevitably becomes a tool that the enemy can use for his own purposes. It is true that the historical lefts have often been defective in this respect – though not always, and much less than it is frequently alleged today. Tito's Yugoslavia, for example, was almost a model for the coexistence of different nationalities on a basis of real equality; but the same certainly cannot be said of Romania. In the third world of Bandung, national liberation movements often succeeded in uniting different ethnic groups and nationalities against the imperialist enemy. But few post-liberation governments were able to handle this diversity democratically and to preserve whatever achievements had been won. Their low propensity to democracy produced as deplorable results in this field as in other problem areas of their societies. When the crisis hit, the ruling classes were powerless to face up to it and often played a key role in fanning communalist withdrawal as a way of maintaining their control of the masses. Even in many real bourgeois democracies, however, it is by no means the case that communal diversity has always been correctly handled. Northern Ireland is the most striking example in this respect.

As we said before, it is failures in the democratic handling of diversity that account for the successes of culturalism. Moreover, amid the thicket of identity demands, there is a democratic criterion that allows us to see and judge each one more lucidly. We may say that a demand is progressive if it links into the struggle against social exploitation and for greater democracy in every dimension, but that it is clearly reactionary, and serves the aims of dominant capital, if it presents itself as 'without a social programme' (on the grounds that this is unimportant), 'not hostile to globalization' (because that too is unimportant) or *a fortiori* alien to the idea of democracy (on the grounds that it is 'Western'). Dominant capital itself understands the difference, and supports the second kind of demand, even when the media profit from its barbaric content to denounce the peoples who are its victims. The idea is always to use or manipulate the movements that raise such demands.

The humanist alternative to worldwide apartheid cannot feed on nostalgic delusions, nor base itself on affirmations of a diversity inherited from the past. It will be effective only if its perspective remains open to the future, only if it seeks to go beyond the truncated and polarizing capitalist form of globalization and to construct a new, post-capitalist form based on real equality among peoples, communities, states and individuals.

Inherited diversities are not a problem because they exist. But, if one becomes fixated on them, one loses sight of other, much more interesting diversities that the invention of the future necessarily throws up. The idea of such new diversities flows from the very idea of emancipatory democracy and the always incomplete modernity that goes hand in hand with it. The creative utopias around which popular struggles for equality and justice may crystallize always find their legitimacy in multiple systems of values, and their necessary complement – systems of social analysis – draw inspiration from equally diverse social theories. Nor can the strategies for real progress in the agreed direction be the monopoly of any one organization. All such diversities in the invention of the future are not only inevitable but welcome.

The alternative to worldwide apartheid is a pluricentric globalization that can ensure different economic and political relations among regions and countries, less unequal and therefore less unfavourable to those which have suffered the most destructive effects of globalization.

To take this road obviously requires complex negotiations and, on that basis, new regulatory systems permitting the accomplishment of development projects worthy of the name. As we saw in the last chapter, this means questioning the present organization of access to markets and capital, of monetary systems, the taxation of natural resources, and moves towards demilitarization.

This perspective reconciling globalization with local and regional autonomy (what I call a delinking consistent with the new challenges) leaves room for a major review of democratization concepts within the UN system, which might then seriously take up the goals of disarmament (on the basis of formulas for national and regional security associated with regional reconstruction), begin the work of establishing global taxation (in connection with management of the earth's natural resources), and help to crown the UN, as the inter-state organization, by starting work towards a 'world parliament' capable of harmonizing the demands of universalism (the rights of individuals, collectives and peoples, political and social rights, etc.) with the diversity of historical and cultural legacies.

Of course, this whole 'project' has a chance of gradual fulfilment only if social forces and projects first take shape at national level as a vehicle for the necessary reforms (which are impossible within the framework of neoliberalism and a polarizing globalization). Thus, whether it is a question of sectoral reforms (state administration, revenue system, education, formulas for sustained involvement in development) or of a more general democratization of societies and their political or economic management, there will be an inescapable need for preliminary stages. Otherwise, the vision of new forms of organization to lift the planet out of chaos and crisis, and to get development moving again, are bound to remain entirely utopian.

In this light, some room must be given to proposals for immediate action capable of mobilizing real political and social forces – first of all at local level, even if the aim is a broader one of 'globalizing struggles'. A long series of regulatory approaches could be rapidly introduced in every field: in the economy (taxation of financial transfers, abolition of tax havens, debt cancellation, etc.), in ecology (species protection, a ban on harmful products and methods, moves towards global consumption taxes on certain non-renewable resources), in social matters (labour legislation, investment codes, participation of peoples' representatives in international bodies), in politics (democracy and individual rights) and in culture (rejection of the commodification of cultural goods).

The medium-term programme I have suggested does not seek only to make market regulation serve the protection of the weak (classes and nations). Its political side is no less important. The key ideas underlying the programme concern disarmament and the drafting of new international law relating to individuals, peoples and states.

In conclusion, the challenge and the responses to it may be summed up in a simple formula: either neoliberal globalization and inevitable apartheid on a world scale, or real negotiations with a view to constructing an alternative, pluricentric globalization.

Four conditions to be satisfied

A genuinely multipolar world will become a reality only when the following four conditions have been satisfied.

1. Real advances towards a different, 'social' Europe, and hence a Europe that has begun to disengage from its imperialist past and present and to embark on the long transition to world socialism. Evidently this implies more than a mere exit from Atlanticism and extreme neoliberalism.
2. The prevalence of 'market socialism' in China over the strong tendencies to an illusory construction of 'national capitalism', which would be impossible to stabilize because it would exclude the majority of workers and peasants.
3. Success of the countries of the South (peoples and states) in rebuilding a 'common front'. This is also essential to provide the leeway for popular classes to impose 'concessions' in their favour and to transform existing systems of rule, replacing the dominant comprador blocs with new 'national, popular and democratic' blocs.
4. Advances at the level of national and international legal systems, harmonizing respect for national sovereignty (including moves from state to popular sovereignty) with respect for all individual and collective, political and social rights.

Bearing in mind the analyses put forward in this book, we can measure the distance between the above four conditions and the present state of struggles and objectives. This gives us a clearer idea of the obstacles that will need to be overcome.

The Europe of governments has not embarked on the road that is required, and popular social and political movements are far from having sized up the challenge. To put it simply, what Europe needs to do is stop investing its surplus capital on the New York finance markets – a practice that enables the United States to overcome its main handicap (the savings deficit) and to pursue its hegemonist offensive. A political way of running the euro, in contrast to that stipulated by existing agreements, is impossible without a European political authority, which in turn is unthinkable so long as the forces ranged behind Atlanticism and neoliberalism dominate the horizon. This being so, there appears to be no threat to the monopoly of what I call the oil dollar standard (which links the dollar, as the only really international currency, to Washington's largely military control of the main oil-producing regions in the Middle East and the Gulf of Guinea). Europe succumbs to the pressure to fall into line behind Washington's policies towards Russia, China, the Arab world and Africa, and 'society' often assists this by badly formulating questions concerning the democratic deficit in those countries and regions. That deficit is real enough, but European public opinion will not help to overcome it by steering in the wake of the United States (a country wrongly seen as wanting to bring about democracy elsewhere), or by echoing the campaigns in Washington on such issues as political liberties in China, the fate of Sinkiang and Tibet, the record of Arab and African autocracies, or the (legitimate) goals of Russia and accusations that it is seeking to 'rebuild' the USSR. Faced with the cynical and manipulative scheming of the United States, a carefully formulated programme is required to bring closer together all the peoples who are the victim of Washington's unacceptable practices and its drive for hegemonic power. But we are still a long way from such a programme. Had the draft European constitution been adopted, setting in stone the neoliberal–Atlanticist option, it would have pointed to nothing good, any more than did the rallying of the socialists to social-liberalism. Far from becoming more pronounced, the clash of political cultures that could lead to a renewal of the European left threatens to be gradually eroded by the Americanization of European thinking.

China, for its part, has opted for a low profile on the world stage; the government is sure of itself and thinks it can manoeuvre internationally without having to side with one or another camp. In the short term, China finances its imports with the dollars it earns from a sizeable trade surplus with the United States, thereby helping to support the dollar standard. Internally, workers' struggles certainly do exist, and despite the autocratic nature of the regime the semi-organized resistance of the peasant majority has up to now succeeded in frustrating attempts to privatize access to the land. On the other hand, the attractiveness of the 'American model' for the new middle classes holds a certain danger for the future political culture of this great country.

In eastern Europe and the countries of the former Soviet Union, the horizon still appears gloomy. High levels of discontent and visible signs of pessimism tend to foster either nostalgia for the Soviet past or devastating illusions about 'Western-style democracy'. No post-Soviet left seems close to making a breakthrough. The 'social movements' most in evidence, which occasionally push forward to centre stage, are manipulated with little difficulty by Washington's intermediaries in the region – as we have seen in Georgia and Ukraine.

In the South, the obstacles are no less significant. Brutal repression is still widespread in much of Asia and Africa, and at this level Latin America enjoys the undeniable advantage that popular attachment to democracy would not make it easy to return to dictatorial practices. Nevertheless, against a backdrop of neoliberalism, this attachment to democracy has become more vulnerable in recent years. In Asia and Africa, a lack of democratic roots means that backward-looking nostalgia often gains ground. Nor should we forget that the 'social movements' which mobilize most people, and enjoy the friendly neutrality of a majority of the population, are the reactionary religious and ethnic fundamentalisms. The social struggles of dominated classes (often expressed in violent explosions), as well as the women's and other progressive and democratic movements, do not make much headway in rolling back regressive ideological illusions.

There are some signs that governments themselves may be coming to question the neoliberal order, especially with regard to the control of capital movements and foreign investment; the triad has recently failed on a number of occasions to impose its point of view on the WTO. Once again, however, there is still a long way to go before we see moves towards a much-needed break. To remove agriculture from the WTO agenda is one indispensable condition for a meaningful turnaround, but this is not yet on the agenda, and governments in the South remain content to do battle on adjacent issues such as the North's subsidization of its agricultural exports. There are not even the beginnings of a worldwide campaign for recognition of all peasants' right of access to the land, in all three continents. Nor are there any plans to abolish the external debt and push through proper international laws on the issue, even among many of those who rightly denounce the criminal injustice of making debt service a priority. The best governments, which, as in the case of Lula in Brazil, have sprung from recent waves of struggle, are still amazingly timid. Will Chávez manage to shape adequate forms of political organization around his intended radical reforms?

The common front of the South certainly does not exist yet, even if there are some signs that one might be reconstituted. The existing regional institutions, designed for the very different purpose of serving as agencies of neoliberal globalization, are unsuited to confronting the real challenges; most of them, especially in Africa and the Arab world, have anyway proved to be little more than façades. South America's Mercosur, which is presented as a model of its kind capable of thwarting Washington's Free Trade Area of the Americas (FTAA) project, remains too limited as a result of its semi-liberal 'common market' orientation. The recent formation of the Group of 20 within the WTO (spurred on by Brazil, India, South Africa and China) is still an ambiguous development. Brazil, whose modernized *latifundia* enjoy cheap labour and huge reserves of land, is the country that stands to gain most from the marketization of agriculture – which means that it does not have the same interests in this field as the countries of Asia.

Need we add that, although public opinion, especially in the West, thankfully managed to repel some of the extreme curtailments of peoples' rights (such as the Multilateral Agreement on Investment, MAI), it was not able to block the adoption of principles which, at the WTO, gave precedence to business law over the rights of peoples? Or that discussion of a reform of the UN, when it takes place at all, points in the opposite direction from our proposals: towards a further taming of the organization and a reduction of its role?

The great strength of the global 'movement'

In contrast to the pessimistic note that the above remarks might strike, we should also note the huge victory already scored by the global 'movement'. 'The world is not for sale' and 'Another world is possible' are not empty phrases but watchwords that have already won public sympathy throughout the world.

The strength of the 'movement' in question lies precisely in its multiplicity, even if this makes more difficult a convergence around strategic priorities. Winning major battles on precise issues, at national, regional and global levels, is the only way of achieving irreversible advances in the fight for 'a better world'. This requires profound and systematic debate, a clear choice of objectives and the organization of appropriate campaigns of action. The mere accumulation of demands by victims of the system, though perfectly legitimate, does not constitute either an alternative (which calls for political coherence) or even a strategy for advance. The 'movement' is in great danger of remaining where it is, and some even try to justify that as a principled option.

The multiplicity exists above all at the level of objectives and, behind them, social interests. The 'movement' now mobilizes sizeable sections of the educated middle classes, especially in the core countries of the system. Their organizations are always centred on one particular objective (the advancement of women, respect for the environment and ecological balance, defence of cultural 'minorities' and other oppressed layers, the winning of certain rights), or are constructed to wage one clearly defined battle. Often they are 'cross-class' organizations by their very nature. We should rejoice at this positive transformation in the activity of social layers which in the past would have merely used their right to vote and the instruments of representative democracy (lobbying, approaches to political parties and parliamentary deputies). Defence of 'the individual' (or individual freedom of initiative), together with the strong moral dimension of many of these movements, is not a 'petty-bourgeois deviation' – as a certain tradition in the workers' movement often used to see it – but an advance in political practice, to the long-term benefit of all the dominated classes.

The fact remains, however, that the new movements have not conjured away the struggles of popular classes for their 'material' interests. Workers' struggles for employment, higher wages and job security, farmers' struggles for decent prices or access to the land and the means to cultivate it, are still the core of the fight to modify the social relationship of forces. Yet it is not always as widely accepted as it should be that labour unions and peasant organizations are essential components of the movement.

For, at the 'great bazaars' that bring the movements together, the middle classes too often take centre stage. No doubt the 'classical' organizations through which the dominated classes act and express themselves are far from being adapted to the new challenges. Changes that the evolution of capitalism has wrought in the organization of work and the management of economic life necessitate changes in the forms of organization and struggle of workers' and peasants' movements; I have discussed these elsewhere, and they are central to the agenda of the World Social Forum. But these necessities do not justify the contempt in which many of the others hold the 'traditional' labour unions and peasant organizations.

For all, the chances of success depend on a large number of factors. One is the capacity to mobilize the 'know-how' of activists to analyse, as experts, the nature of the problems, to work out strategies and tactics, to gain access to the media, and to conduct negotiations. Once again, mobilization of these capacities requires a revision of traditions based on past experience that objective social changes have rendered obsolete. But success – or failure – also depends on the economic and political conjuncture and the sharpness of conflicts within the systems of rule. This is why the 'movement' manifests itself in successive waves of rise and decline, and also why constant analysis of the conjuncture remains an indispensable task.

In general, forms of activism are undergoing change. Some say that involvement tends to be less 'intense' or less 'ongoing', but I am not convinced of this. What I do think – and this is a positive trend – is that people who get involved demand greater respect for the diversity of opinions and democratic practices ('mistrust of leaders', then).

The expansion of the movement has given a voice to many who previously had none – that is, the most deprived and the most disregarded by the institutions of representative democracy. To make their presence felt, these voiceless layers (for example, 'illegal' immigrants or people regarded as 'deviant' by conventional morality) have often needed the support of 'personalities' or activists from backgrounds other than their own. There is no reason to be offended by this, even if the handling of the relationship between the two is always problematic.

A social movement does not mobilize only progressive forces: there are some strong and thoroughly reactionary movements that are not working to build a 'different' (for example, a multipolar) world. In the

United States, labour unions have nearly always defended the imperialist policy of the administration, and had relations with the CIA no less close than those which bound the Soviet unions to their regime. In the United States, 'patriotic associations' or 'sects' still have memberships in the millions, while in Europe the obscurantist offensive of communalist and para-religious movements is making some progress. In some regions of the periphery, para-religious or ethnicist fundamentalism occupies the centre of the stage.

Social movements have considerable difficulty crossing state frontiers: only those who naively believe in a 'global village' or undefined 'multitudes' will be surprised by this. For problems and challenges are specific to each of the countries on earth. The interests of Chinese peasants – who defend their now threatened equal right of access to the land – do not have much in common with the interests of 'competitive' farmers elsewhere. Even within the EU, mere trade-union coordination remains out of reach because of the still decisive weight of the social liberalism of the socialist parties.

How are all these obstacles to be overcome? I see no other way than the organization of broad global campaigns around a number of strategic priorities. I shall simply mention a few examples here for the sake of discussion: (i) a campaign against American 'preventive' wars and for the closure of all US foreign bases ('US Go Home!'); (ii) a campaign for the right of access to the land, which is vitally important to 3 billion peasants in three continents; (iii) a campaign for the regulation of industrial outsourcing; (iv) a campaign for the cancellation of third world external debts. Other proposals are welcome. None of these campaigns will involve 'everyone': the centre of gravity will differ from one campaign to the next, but all should have a strong echo not only in the countries directly concerned but also in others. This will make it possible to find ever more concrete expressions for a new internationalism of the peoples.

In my view, the main danger weighing on the 'movement' is the naive belief that it is possible to change the world without seeking to win power. It is true that, at certain moments in history, powerful social movements have succeeded in 'changing society'. The most recent example of this is 1968, which changed many things for the good in the West: to mention just two, it brought the rise of women's demands and a deepening of individual democratic responsibility. But capitalism showed that it was capable of absorbing such tendencies without having to face a challenge to its fundamental modes of exploitation and oppression. Today the writings of a Castells or Negri propose lending scientific legitimacy to this call to do nothing in the end, on the grounds that everything will be done 'naturally' by itself.

By contrast, it remains centrally important to discuss what is needed to carry the social movement forward, since the movement must become the political force promoting change in the social relationship of forces and, therefore, in the systems of rule. There is not a shadow of doubt that this requires the invention of a 'different kind of politics', but such a formulation is too vague to be anything other than hollow.

The social forums are today confronted with a decisive choice. They can become the sites for the patient construction of new fronts, with the capacity to foster the convergence in diversity of all the progressive forces on earth. To this end, I would propose the working out of joint platforms that reject both neoliberalism and the US-controlled militarization of globalization. A broad, open alliance of movements within this perspective would make it possible to place the emphasis on the construction of positive alternatives. So far as I am concerned, it goes without saying that this excludes reactionary social movements – which implies an end to the ambiguous attitudes that major sections of the left display towards them, since otherwise the social forums will become bazaars from which not much can be expected. The dominant system naturally encourages trends in that direction, which allow it to claim that it is playing the game of democracy. But the democracy to which this would lead is an impotent democracy, incapable of producing alternative political strategies that are coherent and effective. And that can only serve to strengthen the power of the system.

Multipolarity in the twentieth century

The Old World systems were nearly always multipolar, although up to now multipolarity has never been truly general or equal. Thus, hegemony has always been more an objective pursued by the powerful than an actual reality. When hegemony has existed, it has always been relative and provisional.

The partners in the multipolar world of the nineteenth century (which continued until 1945) were scarcely anything other than the 'powers' of their age. Within the contemporary triad, there are probably some who hanker after those times and their characteristic 'balance of power'. But that is not the multipolarity which most of the people on earth (85 per cent) would like to see.

The multipolar world ushered in by the Russian Revolution, then partly imposed by the Asian and African liberation movements, was of a quite different nature. The conventional analysis of the period after the Second World War, which speaks of it in terms of 'bipolarity' and 'cold war', does not give due recognition to the advances of the South. My own approach places the multipolarity of the time in the framework of the real clash of civilizations, which, beyond the deforming ideological expressions, concerned the conflict between capitalism and its possible overcoming by socialism. Whether or not they had made a socialist revolution, the striving of the peoples of the periphery to abolish the effects of polarization due to capitalist expansion necessarily inserted itself into an anti-capitalist perspective.

This is why the reading I shall propose here centres on the strong political solidarity that the conflict between capitalism and socialism inspired, which in turn governed the conceptions of multipolarity peculiar to the second half of the twentieth century.

The drama of the great revolutions

The 'great revolutions' stand out because they projected themselves far into the future, unlike 'ordinary revolutions', which merely respond to the need for change on the immediate agenda.

In the modern era, only three major revolutions may be considered great in this sense – the French, the Russian and the Chinese; while comparable revolutions occurred on a smaller scale in Mexico, Yugoslavia, Vietnam and Cuba. The French Revolution was not only a 'bourgeois revolution' that substituted the capitalist order for the *ancien régime* and bourgeois power for the power of the aristocracy; it was also a people's (especially a peasants') revolution, whose demands challenged the bourgeois order itself. The radical democratic and secular republic, which set itself the ideal of spreading small-scale property to all, did not stem from the mere logic of capital accumulation (based on inequality), but negated that logic and clearly said as much by declaring economic liberalism to be the enemy of democracy. In this sense, the French Revolution already contained the seeds of the socialist revolutions to come, whose 'objective' preconditions evidently did not exist in France at the time (as the fate of Babeuf and his followers showed). The Russian and Chinese revolutions, with which those of Vietnam and Cuba may also be associated, set themselves the goal of communism, although that too was ahead of the objective requirement to solve the immediate problems of the societies in question.

Consequently, all the great revolutions suffered the effects of being ahead of their time and had great difficulty stabilizing themselves; their brief moments of radicalism were succeeded by retreats and reactionary restorations. By contrast, the other revolutions (such as those in England and the United States) heralded a calm and stable deployment of the system, merely registering the requirements of social and political relations already established within the framework of nascent capitalism. In fact, they do not really deserve the name 'revolutions', so striking were their compromises with the forces of the past and their lack of vision for a more distant future.

In spite of their 'defeats', the great revolutions made history – if we consider their long-term impact. By virtue of the avant-garde values defining their project, they enabled creative utopias to seek to win over people's minds and, in the end, to achieve the highest goal of modernity: to make human beings the active subjects of their history. These values contrast with those of the bourgeois order established elsewhere, which, by fostering passive adaptation to the supposedly objective requirements of the deployment of capital, gave full force to the economistic alienation underlying such adaptation.

The weight of imperialism, the permanent stage of the global expansion of capitalism

Since its inception, and at every stage in its history, the global deployment of capitalism has always been polarizing. Yet this characteristic of actually existing capitalism has always been underestimated, to say the least, because of the Eurocentrism dominating modern thought, even in the avant-garde ideological formations peculiar to the great revolutions. The historical Marxism of the successive Internationals only partly escaped this general rule.

To understand the immensity of this imperialist reality, and to draw all the strategic consequences for the changing of the world, is the first indispensable task that all social and political forces on the receiving end of it have to face, in both the core and the periphery. For what imperialism has brought about is not so much a maturing of conditions for 'socialist revolutions' (or accelerated tendencies in that direction) in the centres of the world system, as challenges to its order through revolts in the periphery. It is no accident that Russia was the 'weak link' in the system in 1917, or that revolution in the name of socialism then shifted eastward to China and elsewhere, whereas the collapse in the West on which Lenin pinned his hopes failed to materialize. The countries that underwent revolution therefore faced the dual, contradictory task of 'catching up' (with methods similar to those of capitalism) and 'doing something else' ('building socialism'). This combination turned out as it did in the various countries; it might perhaps have been better, in the sense of allowing communist aspirations to grow stronger as advances were made in catching up. In any event, this real contradiction crucially shaped the objective conditions under which the post-revolutionary societies evolved.

The forms of political action and organization developed by 'revolutionary parties' (in this case, the Communists of the Third International) remained trapped in the idea that the revolution was 'imminent', that the 'objective conditions' for it were present. The Party therefore had to make up for what was lacking: it had to become an organization to 'make the revolution', and therefore, under the circumstances, to stress homogeneity (later 'monolithism') and an almost military discipline. The parties in question maintained these forms of organization, even when the perspective of an immediate revolutionary assault was abandoned in the late 1920s. They were then placed in the service of a quite different objective: protection of the Soviet state, both internally and externally.

In the peripheries of globalized capitalism – by definition, the 'storm zone' in the imperialist system – a form of revolution did remain on the agenda. But its objective was still essentially blurred and ambiguous. Was it national liberation from imperialism (and preservation of much, or even most, of the social relations characteristic of capitalist modernity), or was it something more? Both in the radical revolutions of China, Vietnam and Cuba, and in the less radical ones in Asia, Africa and Latin America, the question was still: 'to catch up' or 'to do something else'? This challenge was in turn linked to another priority task: defence of the encircled Soviet Union.

Defence of the post-revolutionary states central to the vanguard's strategic choices

The Soviet Union, and later China, found themselves confronted with a dominant capitalism and Western powers systematically seeking to isolate them. Let us just recall that, for a third of the short history of the United States, the strategy of this hegemonic power of the capitalist system has focused on the goal of destroying its two enemies, whether truly socialist or not; and that Washington has managed to draw into this strategy its subaltern allies in the other centres of the triad (Europe and Japan) and the countries of the periphery, gradually substituting the rule of comprador classes for that of classes with roots in the people's liberation movement.

It is easy to understand that, since revolution was not on the immediate agenda elsewhere, priority was usually given to defence of the post-revolutionary states. This became the central issue shaping political strategy – in the Soviet Union under Lenin and then Stalin and his successors, in Maoist and post-Maoist China, in the national-populist regimes of Asia and Africa, and among the Communist vanguards (whether lined up behind Moscow or Beijing or neither).

The Soviet Union and China experienced the vicissitudes of a great revolution at the same time that they faced the consequences of the uneven expansion of world capitalism. Both post-revolutionary regimes gradually sacrificed their original objectives to the immediate requirements of 'catching up' – a slide which, by substituting state management for Marx's communist goal of social ownership and by using brutal (sometimes bloody) dictatorial methods to stifle popular democracy, paved the way for the later rush towards capitalist restoration that is common to the two countries (despite the different roads they have travelled). The instruments deployed internally for 'defence of the post-revolutionary state' went hand in hand with external strategies that prioritized the same goal. Communist parties were asked to line up behind these choices, not only in their general strategic direction but even in their day-to-day tactical adjustments. This could not fail to produce a rapid weakening of their capacity for critical thought, as abstract talk of revolution (still supposedly 'imminent') and the maintenance of quasi-military forms of organization come hell or high water detached them from analysis of the real contradictions of society.

The vanguards that refused such a crippling alignment, in some cases daring to look the post-revolutionary societies in the face, did not give up the original Leninist hypothesis of the imminence of revolution, even though it had been ever more visibly refuted in reality. This was the case with Trotskyism and the parties of the Fourth International. It was also true of many activist revolutionary organizations: from the Philippines to India (Naxalites inspired by Maoism), and from the Arab world (Arab nationalists and their followers in South Yemen) to Latin America (Guevarism).

Nation-building and/or socialist construction in the radical countries of the periphery

The great national liberation movements of Asia and Africa that came into open conflict with the imperialist order, like those that led revolutions in the name of socialism, had to face the conflicting demands of 'catching up' ('nation-building') and transforming social relations in favour of the popular classes. With regard to the second of these tasks, the 'post-revolutionary' (or simply post-independence) regimes of Asia and Africa were certainly less radical than the Communist regimes – which is why I call them 'national-populist'. Sometimes they drew inspiration from organizational forms (single party, undemocratic rule, a state-run economy) that had been developed in the experiences of 'actually existing socialism', but they generally watered them down through vague ideological choices and compromises with the past.

These were the conditions under which the regimes in place, as well as the critical vanguards (historical Communism), were asked to support the Soviet Union (or, more rarely, China) and invited to enjoy its support. The constitution of this common front against the imperialist aggression of the United States and its European and Japanese partners was certainly beneficial to the peoples of Asia and Africa; it created a degree of autonomy both for the initiatives of their ruling classes and for the activity of popular classes. The proof of this is what happened subsequently, after the Soviet collapse. Even before it, those ruling classes which opted for 'the West' on the illusory grounds that this would be favourable to them obtained nothing in the end. (In Sadat's Egypt, the main case in point, the calculation was that a friendly United States, holding nearly all the cards on the Palestinian issue, could turn the situation round in favour of the Arab and Palestinian cause!) Indeed, their capitulation encouraged the deployment of the strategic offensives of imperialism and, in the case of Israel, strengthened the Washington–Tel Aviv axis.

This is not to say that Moscow did not impose dubious conditions on political forces that were ranged alongside the popular classes in countries allied to it – and, in particular, on the local Communist parties. One might have thought that, within the anti-imperialist front, these parties would preserve all their autonomy of movement – a recognition of the conflicting interests and social projects among the partners involved in the front. For the ruling classes were ultimately pursuing a capitalist (though also 'national') project, whereas the satisfaction of popular class interests required going beyond a perspective whose narrow limits had already been demonstrated in history. But the fact is that the Soviet state fed the illusions that the national capitalist project carried within it, and thereby undermined the autonomous expression of the popular classes. The invention of a theory of the 'non-capitalist road' expressed this choice.

There can be no doubt that during the Bandung era (1955–75) it was difficult to draw a distinction between the interests of governments and the interests of their peoples. The regimes had only recently emerged out of huge national liberation movements (which had routed imperialism in its old 'colonial' or 'semi-colonial' forms), or sometimes out of genuine revolutions associated with those movements, as in China, Vietnam and Cuba. They were still 'close' to their peoples, and enjoyed great legitimacy.

The example of Arab Communism sheds some light on the tragic consequences of this rallying to the idea of a 'non-capitalist road'. A large majority of Arab Communists accepted the Soviet proposals and became, at best, the 'left wing' of the anti-imperialist national-populist regimes, giving them scarcely critical, virtually unconditional support. Two examples of this were the self-dissolution of the Egyptian Communist Party in 1965, in the deluded hope that it would be allowed to breathe new life into the Nasserite Socialist Party; and the rallying of Khaled Bagdash in Syria to the thesis that only nation-building (not even spelled out as non-capitalist) was the order of the day. I have expressed my views on this elsewhere, most notably at the time when many of the activists of the period were publishing their memoirs in Egypt. I concluded that Arab Communism as a whole had not essentially left the framework of the 'national-populist' project, and had failed to see that in the end this fitted into a strictly capitalist perspective. This was not an 'opportunist' conjunctural orientation on its part, but a structural choice that expressed the original deficiencies of the Communist parties in question, the ambiguity of the ideologies they promoted, and ultimately their ignorance of the popular classes whose immediate and long-term interests they were supposed to be defending. The result of this unfortunate option was a loss of Communist credibility once the national-populist regimes reached their historical limits and suffered an erosion of legitimacy. Since the Communist left had not presented itself as an alternative beyond national populism, a vacuum was created on the political stage that opened the way for the disastrous rise of political Islam.

It is true that small numbers of Arab Communists rejected this un-conditional rallying to the policies of the Soviet state; the examples of the Qawmiyin and their emulators in South Yemen, or a few other 'Maoist' nuclei, bear testimony to this. But they did not depart from the original Leninist thesis that revolution was 'imminent', which they shared with the Guevarist movements of Latin America and the Naxalites in India. The defeat of the courageous movements they inspired shows with hindsight that Lenin's thesis was wrong and based on tragic simplifications.

The no less tragic history of the South African Communist Party forms part of a similar downward slide. In the 1930s the SACP enjoyed the support of a majority of the African popular classes, while the ANC comprised only a minority of the petty bourgeoisie. Yet, on Moscow's advice, the Party wound itself up and offered the leadership of the national movement to the ANC on a platter, with the consequences we know.

In contrast, the Indian Communists, under the influence of Maoism, mostly kept a critical distance from Congress and rejected the thesis of a 'non-capitalist road'. As we have seen in the chapter on India, this is doubtless why they have survived the disaster and are in a better position than others to face the new challenges.

A further contrast is the sizeable fraction of the Latin American left which, under Cuban influence, detached itself from official Communism. The polemics that took place on this occasion – under the banner of the first version of *dependencia* theory – served useful functions and explain, at least in part, why the attachment to democracy has more solid roots there.

Opening debate on the long transition to world socialism

While recognizing Lenin's mistaken view of the real challenges, and his misjudgement of the ripeness for revolution, we need to go beyond criticism and self-criticism of the history of twentieth-century

Communism, by openly and inventively fostering debate on the positive alternative strategies for the twenty-first century.

Here I can do no more than briefly summarize the points I have made elsewhere.

- Strategies must be devised in response to the challenges of the long transition from world capitalism to world socialism.
- In the course of this long transition, social, economic and political systems produced by the struggles of the reproductive elements of capitalist society will combine, in contradictory fashion, with elements tending to initiate and develop socialist social relations. Two conflicting logics will therefore be present, in permanent combination and permanent contradiction with each other.
- Progress in this direction is necessary and possible in all regions of the world capitalist system, both the imperialist centres and the compradorized peripheries. Of course, by force of circumstance, there will have to be concrete and specific intermediate stages, especially with regard to the contrasts between centres and peripheries.
- Social, ideological and political forces expressing, however confusedly, the interests of popular classes are already working in the directions indicated. The so-called 'alter-globalization' movements are material proof of this. But these movements serve as vehicles for different alternatives, some progressive (in the above sense), some deluded or even clearly reactionary (para-fascist responses to the challenges). To politicize the debate – in the true and proper sense of the term – is the sine qua non for building what I call 'convergence in diversity' of the progressive forces.
- The victims of the deployment of neoliberal capitalism are the majority in all parts of the world, and socialism must be capable of mobilizing the new historical opportunity this creates. But it will be able to do this only if it can take account of the changes resulting from the technological revolutions, which have completely altered the social architecture once and for all. Communism must no longer be the banner only of the 'industrial working class', in the old sense of the term; it can become the banner representing the future of the broad majority of working people, despite the diversity of their situations. To rebuild the unity of working people – both those who benefit from a

certain stabilization of the system and those who are excluded from it
– is today a major challenge for the inventive thinking that is needed
for communist renewal. In the peripheries, this also means organizing
huge movements to establish an equal right of access to the land for
the whole peasantry. Renewal is all the more necessary because it
has often been forgotten that the peasantry is still a half of humanity,
and that capitalism in all its forms is incapable of solving this major
problem.

• An effective strategy for action within this perspective must be capable
of producing simultaneous advances in three directions: social progress,
democratization and the construction of a pluricentric world system.
The political democracy usually proposed as an accompaniment to the
economic options of liberal capitalism is destined to strip democracy
of all credibility, in quite dramatic ways. At the same time, social
progress from the top down is no longer acceptable as a substitute for
inventive formulas involving the democratic power of popular classes.
There will be no socialism without democracy, but also no democratic
advances without social progress. Lastly, in view of the persistence of
national diversity and the political cultures shaping it, as well as the
inequality historically produced by the deployment of world capitalism, it is clear that a margin of opportunity for the necessary social
and democratic advances will require the construction of a pluricentric
world system. And the first condition for this, of course, is to defeat
Washington's project for military control of the planet.

Further reading

This work focuses on the geopolitics of certain major issues – a deliberate choice on my part, motivated by the fact that the 'social movements' of our time shy away from this dimension. Geopolitics is part of 'politics'. But the social movements generally believe that politics is 'bad', that nothing good can come of it, and that we need to dissociate ourselves from it in order to change the world. Some have tried to give a theoretical justification for this attitude, which in my view involves a failure to assume the necessary responsibilities. If 'politics' is bad, the solution is not to abolish it – which is anyway an impossibility – but to engage in 'good politics'. The reader will certainly be able to gauge the distance between my own geopolitical analysis and more conventional approaches. I have always stressed that the distinctive logics of social (and hence political) systems are closely linked to those governing the current or projected forms of globalization. However, given my focus here on geopolitical aspects, only passing reference has been made to their relationship with social systems. I would therefore like to add a few further points by way of suggestions for further reading.

On the nature of actually existing capitalism

1. The critique of 'pure economics' (the economics of an imaginary capitalist system), and the requirements for a political economy of 'actually existing capitalism' (what I call 'underdetermination' in history). A

critical reading of liberal ideology, identification of the limits of market socialization (as opposed to socialization through democracy).

- Pure economics or the witchcraft of the contemporary world: Samir Amin, *Spectres of Capitalism*, Monthly Review Press, New York, 1998, ch. 8.
- Overdetermination/underdetermination in history: *Spectres of Capitalism*, ch. 3.
- Liberal ideology: Samir Amin, *The Liberal Virus*, London: Pluto, 2004, pp. 13–19.
- Low-intensity democracy, market socialization or socialization through democracy: *The Liberal Virus*, pp. 42–51.

2. The imperialist dimension of the global expansion of capitalism.

- The successive phases of imperialist expansion and the main features of the core–periphery relations resulting from it: Samir Amin, *Capitalism in the Age of Globalization*, Zed Books, London, 1997, ch. 1.
- The new stage of imperialism now under construction; the core's five new monopolies. The analysis here refutes the concept of 'emergent economies', which in fact are merely tomorrow's peripheral countries: *Capitalism in the Age of Globalization*, ch. 1, pp. 3–5.
- The distinction between the value form, the law of value in general and the 'globalized' law of value, in the various stages of the global expansion of capitalism: *Capitalism in the Age of Globalization*, ch. 1, pp. 3–5.
- The main ideological expressions in the political economy of capitalism; actually existing imperialism in the successive stages of its deployment: *Spectres of Capitalism*, ch. 3.
- The recent formation of a 'collective Triad imperialism' (USA + Europe + Japan) and the instruments of its economic and political management: Samir Amin, *Obsolescent Capitalism*, Zed Books, London, 2003.

On the transformation of contemporary capitalism and the critique of mainstream discourse

1. A critique of postmodernist ideas concerning labour, value, technological revolution and 'cognitive' capitalism, the dominance of finance and 'patrimonial' capitalism.

The scope of the present technological revolution, as well as its effects on labour and the law of value, are the theme of a copious literature. The dominant theorists claim that 'horizontal' or 'networked' social relations have been replacing hierarchical relations, that 'knowledge' has become the most important factor of production, and that 'old theories' of labour and value (those of Marx, naturally) have become obsolete. The main initiator of such thinking is undoubtedly Manuel Castells, whose ideas have recently been taken up by Hardt and Negri.

My own analysis of the transformation of capitalism is quite different. First, it puts into a proper perspective the observations that are given such prominence in mainstream discourses, which as a matter of fact concern only parts of society in the imperialist core. Second, the importance of knowledge for the efficiency of productive systems is not a new discovery. Third and last, the social relations of subordination between labour and capital are still in place (capital continues to employ labour, and we are not at all heading for a reversal whereby labour makes use of capital); this completely nullifies postmodernist discourse on the matter.

My analysis underlines other major features of the ongoing trans-formations: the five monopolies of the core, the reversed ratio of dead capital to living labour in some sectors of the 'new economy'. On this basis, I propose a redefinition of the content of the globalized law of value and the forms of the exploitation of labour.

Mainstream discourse also emphasizes the dominant position of finance within the system, claiming that this expresses a lasting quali-tative change on the basis of which a new 'patrimonial' capitalism is taking shape. In my view, this 'financialization' is a characteristic of the transition crisis, and in this light 'patrimonial capitalism' can be seen for what it really is: just a pretentious formulation for the old myth of a 'people's capitalism'.

Samir Amin, *Obsolescent Capitalism*, ch. 6; Samir Amin, *Spectres of Capitalism*, ch. 5.

Samir Amin, 'Globalism or Apartheid on a Global Scale', in I. Wallerstein, ed., *The Modern World System in the Longue Durée*, Paradigm, Boulder, CO, 2004.

Samir Amin, *Technological Revolution and Cognitive Capitalism*, forthcoming.

2. In connection with the changes in contemporary capitalism, I have also proposed:

- a critique of the concept of globalization; a review of earlier, pre-modern forms of globalization (*Capitalism in the Age of Globalization*, chs 1 & 2; and 'The Ancient World System versus the Modern World System', *Review*, vol. 14, 1991, pp. 349–86);
- a critique of the language of contemporary mainstream discourse: civil society, governance, communities, poverty, consensus, alternation, and so on.

On contradictions within the contemporary triad

1. US hegemony: established fact or just an ambition of the American ruling class? An expression of real economic strength or, on the contrary, a means of compensating for serious weaknesses? The militarization of globalization, successive 'preventive wars' and the 'empire of chaos' (an expression I have been using since 1990). What can be expected of the American people?

Samir Amin, *Obsolescent Capitalism*, ch. 5.
Bill Fletcher, 'Can US Workers Embrace Anti-Imperialism?', in J.B. Foster, ed., *Pax Americana*, Monthly Review Press, New York, 2004.
PNAC, *Project for the New American Century*, Washington DC, 1997.
The National Security Strategy, Washington DC, 2002.

2. The fading of the European project (is it to be a European project or the European part of the American project?). Roots and possible directions of the clash of political cultures.

Samir Amin, *Obsolescent Capitalism*, pp. 101–6.
Samir Amin, *The Liberal Virus*, pp. 62–106.
Samir Amin, 'Judaïsme, Christianisme, Islam', *Social Compass*, vol. 46, no. 4, 1999, pp. 545–60; partly translated as 'The Theocratic Tempta-tion: Judaism, Christianity, Islam', *Dialectic, Cosmos and Society* 12, Spring 1999, pp. 5–12.
Marie-Thérèse Bitsch, *Histoire de la construction européenne*, Complexe, Paris, 2004.

On the socialist perspective and the critique of 'actually existing socialisms'

1. However varied the visions of socialism, all may perhaps agree that collective choices cannot just 'spontaneously' result from individual choices (as liberal ideology asserts), that they must therefore be collectively worked out through the deepening of democracy, and that they have no meaning except within the perspective of an ever greater affirmation of equality. Socialism, then, is synonymous with emancipation and equality, and calls for democratic management of politics and the economy. This definition, which I share with others (see, e.g., Tony Andréani, *Le socialisme est (a)venir*, 2 vols, Syllepse, Paris, 2004), requires in turn that we identify the strategic stages necessary for the construction of socialism on a world scale, through a 'long transition' in the course of which the forms and values governing capitalist reproduction will be conflictually combined with other forms and values associated with the logic of socialism.

In this perspective, we may conceive of a 'market socialism' that combines democratic regulation of the market with methods of planning that are themselves the result of democratic debate rather than technocratic command. Such a market socialism (or 'socialism with the market', as Tony Andréani puts it) may be thought of as constituting a transitional stage; we shall return in a moment to current Chinese experiences in this connection. This opens up debate on the socialism that might lie further ahead in the future, and on the place that the 'market' might occupy within it – a debate that evidently calls for fresh appraisal of Marxist and other theories of alienation.

Furthermore, the perspective of socialism has no meaning unless it is 'global'; visions of socialism reserved for the economically most advanced countries (15 per cent of the world's population) are little different from the perspective of 'apartheid on a world scale' characteristic of imperialist capitalism. Up until now, the 'need for socialism' has forcefully asserted itself in the peripheries of the system, through revolutions conducted in the name of socialism and through the radicalization of national liberation movements (see Appendix 1).

The problems of 'inherited' cultural diversity, as well as the diversity of future-oriented conceptions of socialism, should also be addressed in this context.

- Samir Amin, *Capitalism in the Age of Globalization*, ch. 11 and conclusion. In the conclusion to *Class and Nation* (Monthly Review Press, New York, 1980), I had already outlined the alternative facing the world: either capitalism ending in chaos, or a controlled transition beyond capitalism.
- *Spectres of Capitalism*, ch. 4 (on communism as bearer and product of a new culture) and ch. 5 (on the contradictory withering away of the law of value, with a potential for the construction of socialist social relations but also for the slide of capitalism towards a new type of 'tributary empire' underpinning apartheid on a world scale).
- The challenges of modernity: *Obsolescent Capitalism*, Appendix 1.
- The distinction between inherited diversity and diversity concerning the invention of the future: *Obsolescent Capitalism*, Appendix 7.
- The debate on market socialism: see below, on Sovietism and the Chinese experience.
- The centrality of the new challenges facing the movement towards socialism (the right to the land for the world's peasantry, the construction of united labour fronts, the forging of solidarity among the peoples of the periphery, the building of people's sovereignty): see below.

2. Critique of the experiences of 'actually existing socialism' cannot abstract from the historical conditions of the countries in question (Russia, China, Vietnam, Cuba).

Russia

Samir Amin, 'La Russie, géographie ou histoire', ch. 8 of *Les Défis de la mondialisation*, L'Harmattan, Paris, 1996.

Samir Amin, *Re-reading the Postwar Period*, Monthly Review Press, New York, 1997, ch. 7.

Moshe Lewin, *The Soviet Century*, Verso, London, 2005.

Boris Kagarlitsky, *La Russie aujourd'hui*, Parangon, Paris, 2004.

Frédéric Encel and Olivier Guez, *La Grande alliance*, Flammarion, Paris, 2003.

China, Maoism and market socialism

Samir Amin, *The Future of Maoism*, Monthly Review Press, New York, 1983.

Samir Amin, *Capitalism in an Age of Globalization*.

Samir Amin, 'Post-Maoist China', *Review*, vol. 22, no. 4, 1999, pp. 375–85.

Samir Amin, 'China, Market Socialism, and U.S. Hegemony', *Review*, vol. 28, no. 3, 2005.

Vietnam

Marie Lavigne, *Économie du Viet Nam*, L'Harmattan, Paris, 1999.

Cuong Le Van, ed., *L'économie vietnamienne en transition*, L'Harmattan, Paris, 1998.

Philippe Langlet, ed., *Introduction à l'histoire contemporaine du Viet Nam*, Les Indes Savantes, Paris, 2001.

Rémy Herrera, ed., *Cuba révolutionnaire*, 4 vols, L'Harmattan, Paris, 2003, vol. 1.

Critical analysis of EU policies towards Eastern Europe seems to be virtually non-existent. Yet the logic of EU expansion is, in its main aspects, similar to that of US expansion in Latin America. The silence of the West European left on these issues is disturbing.

On the global insertion of the various regions of 'the South'

Tropical Africa

*   The specificities of African 'underdevelopment': Samir Amin, 'Under-development and Dependence in Black Africa', *Journal of Modern African Studies*, vol. 10, no. 4, 1972, pp. 503–24; Philippe Hugon, *Économie de l'Afrique*, La Découverte, Paris, 2003.
*   On the current projects for Africa's insertion into neoliberal global-ization (Cotonou accords between the ACP group of states and the EU, the Regional Economic Partnership Accords (REPAs), the New Partnership for Africa's Development (NEPAD), etc.): Samir Amin, ed., *L'Afrique, exclusion programmée ou renaissance?*, forthcoming; Jacques Berthelot, 'L'OMC et la question agraire: les principaux pièges contre le Sud', forthcoming.

South Africa

Material supplementing the synthetic analyses in this book: Hein Marais, 'L'integration régionale en Afrique australe', and Langa Zita, 'L'Afrique du Sud est-elle le maillon faible de l'impérialisme?', in Amin, *L'Afrique, exclusion programmée ou renaissance?*

Arab and Islamic worlds

- For my critique of autocracy in the region (the 'Mameluk system'), the failure of the nineteenth-century *Nahda* and the rise of political Islam: Samir Amin and Ali El Kenz, *Europe and the Arab World*, Zed Books, London, 2005, ch. 1; Amin, *Obsolescent Capitalism*, Appendix 6.
- Critique of the projects for 'Euro-Mediterranean dialogue': Samir Amin and Ali El Kenz, *Europe and the Arab World*, chs 3 and 4.

East, South and Southeast Asia

Diana Hochraich et al., eds, *Après la crise, les économies asiatiques face aux défis de la mondialisation*, Karthala, Paris, 2003.

David Camroux, ed., *Tigers in Trouble*, Zed Books, London, 1998.

Central and West Asia

Ali Banuazizi, ed., *The New Geopolitics of Central Asia and Its Borderlands*, Indiana University Press, Bloomington, 1994.

Ahmed Rashid, *The Resurgence of Central Asia*, Zed Books, London, 1994.

Latin America and the Caribbean

- The *desarrollismo* and *dependencia* debates provided material for a number of well-known major works. No less important are the conclusions for political action that the Left drew from them in the region. See Marta Harnecker, *La Gauche à l'aube du XXIe siècle*, Outremont, Quebec: Lanctôt, 1999.
- Identifiable advances have occurred with the coming to power of the Workers' Party in Brazil, Chávez in Venezuela, the neo-Zapatista movement in Mexico, and the mobilizations of the indigenous peoples. Will they measure up to the challenges? Strengths and weaknesses of these early signs of a 'new beginning for Latin America'. On the plus side: democratic demands have stronger roots than in Asia or Africa; there are some signs of regional alternatives to the expansion of the US-dominated common market (Mercosur versus NAFTA), but also of an attachment to 'European culture' and the consumerist model that goes together with it. Strength of reactionary political forces in

the elected institutions (the *latifundistas* in the Brazilian Congress, for example) and the judicial system (an obstacle to reform in Venezuela). See Coral Wynter, 'The Revolutionary Process in Venezuela', *Links* 26, 2004; Pablo G. Casanova, *Las nuevas ciencias y las humanidades, de la academia a la política*, forthcoming; Felipe de J. Perez Cruz, 'El neoliberalismo en Brasil', and Atilio Borón, 'El Alca, más allá de la economía', *Cuadernos de Nuestra América* 33, 2004.

The emergence of 'ethnicism'

Samir Amin, *L'Ethnie à l'assaut des nations*, L'Harmattan, Paris, 1994, on Yugoslavia and Ethiopia; partly in *Capitalism in the Age of Globalization*, ch. 4.

On present conflicts and the geometry of possible alliances

1. Respect for national sovereignty and the military balance of power. Does this necessarily involve 'proliferation', in the absence of organized disarmament of the major powers (primarily the United States)? Critique of the 'right of intervention'. The new issue of people's sovereignty and its democratic foundations. Samir Amin, Jean de Maillard, François Rigaux et al., *Droits marchands, droits des peuples: dérives du droit international*, forthcoming.

2. The new agrarian question, property reform and the right to the land; old debates (Marx and Vera Zasulich; the Second International – Kautsky and Lenin); African debates of the 1950s and 1960s; the need to discuss new issues. Samir Amin, 'Les réformes foncières nécessaires en Asie et en Afrique', forthcoming; and Samir Amin, ed., Part One of *Les luttes paysannes et ouvrières face aux défis du XXIe siècle*, Les Indes Savantes, Paris, 2004.

3. The new issue of building workers' unity, among 'stable' and non-stable sectors. Amin, ed., Part 2 of *Les luttes paysannes et ouvrières face aux défis du XXIe siècle*.

4. The new issue of building solidarity among the peoples of the South. Samir Amin, 'Laying New Foundations for the Solidarity of the Peoples of the South', *Social Sciences Probings*, vol. 15, nos. 3–4, 2003.

5. Some new advances whose scale remains unclear and ambiguous:

- In 2003, at the WTO meeting in Cancún, the countries of the South presented a challenge to the characteristically arrogant 'proposals' of the United States and the European Union (represented by Pascal Lamy) concerning the opening up of the South's agriculture to 'competition'. (An African farmer producing roughly one tonne of grain a year is supposed to compete with those in the USA and Europe producing 1,000 to 2,000 tonnes a year!) But the countries of the South were content to discuss the secondary issue of agricultural export subsidies, and did not dare raise the key demand that agricultural and livestock production should be excluded from the WTO agenda. Samir Amin, 'WTO Recipe for World Hunger', *Ahram Weekly* 657, October 2003.

- At the same WTO meeting, a Group of Twenty led by Brazil, South Africa, India and China showed some signs of taking shape, although its aims remain ambiguous in so far as the *latifundia* of Brazil and South Africa are competitive agri-exporters, while the peasantries of the South do not generally share their interests. Moreover, Brazil and South Africa do not accept that food security needs to be a political priority.

6. The variable geometry of the conflicts in prospect. The Southern 'storm zone'. The persistence of imperialism in new forms goes hand in hand with compradorization of the dominant classes in the periphery. The new comprador bloc in the emergent countries groups together the bosses of dependent industry, technocrats and bureaucrats, the middle classes and sections of the rich peasantry who benefit from expansion. This bloc excludes the peasant and working-class majorities and is therefore incapable of 'stabilization'. It implies that periods of (generally aberrant) democracy will be interspersed with brutal dictatorial backlashes. The ground is also being laid for devastating religious and ethnicist 'fundamentalisms'. The alternative is to construct national popular-democratic blocs, and to ensure that globalization is adjusted to their requirements. Samir Amin, *Obsolescent Capitalism*, pp. 106–12.

Index

accountability, 125
active insertion, 28
Afghanistan, war in, 123
Africa, roots of exclusion of, 92–4
African National Congress (ANC), 96, 97, 172
agrarian question, 40; in Europe, 39
agrarian reform, 65, 70, 71, 76, 93, 97, 152
agriculture, 37–8, 109; disappearance of, 141; marketization of, 160; modernization of, 38, 97 (in China, 40); mechanization of, 38; productivity of, 92; subsidies for, 109, 159; suggested removal from WTO agenda, 159 *see also* peasant agriculture
Algeria, 96
Ali, Mohamed, 98
alter-globalization *see* globalization, alternative
Amazon region, 108
American Revolution, 46
Amin, Samir, *Accumulation on a World Scale*, 2
'another world is possible', 160–62
apartheid, 96, 138; global, 122, 140, 155, 157; invention of, 95
Arab nationalism, 100, 169
Arab world, failed insertion of, 98–102
Argentina, 104, 124
arms, sales of, 128–9
Atlanticism, 11, 14, 22, 26, 57, 61, 112, 147, 149, 158; challenge to, 8

autocratic power: in new Russia, 57–9; in Soviet Russia, 51–2

Baath party, 74
Bandung Conference (1955), 77, 81
Bandung era (1955–75), 84, 113, 150, 171; balance sheet of, 85–92
Bandung project, 104, 106, 107, 154
Bertrand Russell War Crimes Tribunal, 142
Bharatva, 76, 78
Bhopal disaster, 144
Biafra war, 116
bipolarity, 165
Blair, Tony, 16
Bolivia, 104
Brazil, 10, 41, 82, 96, 104, 105, 108, 132, 150, 160
British colonialism, 95; in India, 69–72, 74, 76
Bush administration, 8

capital market, global, construction of, 139
capital transfers, controls on, 108
capitalism: early universalism of, 126; growth of, 119–20; logic of expansion of, 151; national, 47; nature of, 2–5; popular, 34; without capitalists, 90
capitalist road in China *see* China, capitalist road in
Cardoso, F.H., 105
Caribbean, 103–5

Casablanca Group, 86
Caspian Sea, oilfields, 60
caste system in India, 70, 71–2; abolition of, 80
Castells, Manuel, 164; *The Rise of the Network Society*, 153
catching up, 28, 99, 117, 167, 169, 170
chaos: as part of nature, 153; generalization of, 132; of original capitalism, 120
Chávez, Hugo, 104, 105, 160
Chile, 103
China, 10, 62, 68, 69, 75, 81, 82, 108, 148–9, 150, 157, 158–9, 160, 163, 169, 170, 171; as industrial power, 65; as Middle Empire, 44; capitalist road in, 30, 31, 33, 40–41; challenge to the imperialist order, 25–48; encirclement of, 10; growth in, 75–6; national question in, 43; population of, 36; post-Maoist, 26; poverty in, 41; project for dismemberment of, 11, 26; success of peasant revolution in, 42
Chinese Revolution, 26, 30, 39, 75, 166, 167, 168, 169; legacy of, 41
Chung Kuo, 44
civil society, 122, 136, 153; concept of, 21
civil war, 132
clash of civilizations, 123, 126, 165
co-operatives, voluntary, 40
Cold War, 14, 113, 165
collective bargaining, 64
collective ownership, 35
collective triad imperialism, 121
Colombia, 108
colonialism, 92–3; in India, 69–72 *see also* British colonialism, decolonization and neo-colonialism
colonization, models of, 93
commodification: of cultural goods, 156; of social life, 141
common goods, 141
communism, 79, 170; in Arab world, 171–2; in China, 75; in India, 70, 71, 73–4, 78, 79, 80, 172; renewal of, 173–4
Communist Party: of China, 32, 43; of Egypt, 171; of India, 74; of South Africa, 96, 97, 172; of Soviet Union, 58, 59, 66, 168, 169
Communist Party–Marxist (India), 78
communitarianism, 19, 20

comprador class, 43, 63, 77, 79, 80, 129; recompradorization, 106–7
comprador regimes, 45, 46, 57, 150
Congress Party (India), 72, 73, 78; collapse of legitimacy, 79
core–periphery relation, 2, 3, 40
corporatism, in new Russia, 59–60; in Soviet system, 50–51
corruption, 92, 94, 123, 137, 138
crimes against humanity, 115
Cuba, 29, 42, 104, 108, 171
Cuban Revolution, 103, 166, 168
culturalism, 130

Dalits, 71–2, 80; struggles of, 78
debt: external, 110, 136–7, 144; cancellation of, 163; classification of, 137–8; grades of acceptability of, 110; proposed audit of, 137; relief of, 138
debt servicing, 12
decentralization, 125
decolonization, 85
delinking, 27, 85, 91, 98, 156; of the Soviet system, 53–4
demilitarization, 155
democracy, 36, 62, 64, 77, 78, 79, 90, 97, 104–5, 107, 113, 115, 118, 122, 124, 130, 131, 152, 154, 158, 159, 164, 174; as product of modernity, 126; conflict with sovereignty, 128, 133; 'crusade' for, 128; in Latin America, 159; legitimacy of, 124; relation to modernity, 42; strengthening of anti-democracy, 125; Western, 32
democratic responsibility, individual, 163
democratization, 47, 96, 98, 112, 123, 126; within UN, 156
Deng Xiaoping, 28
dependencia theory, 172
dependency school, 103
desarrollismo, 103, 104, 115
development, 117; ideology of, 86; imposition of, 89; model of, 103; right to, 134; sustainable, 140
development decades, 84
dictatorship, 118; of the proletariat, 32
disarmament, 129, 156, 157; role of UN in, 133
distribution of wealth, 74, 75, 96, 97, 110
diversity, 156; convergence in, 173; respect for, 130, 152, 154, 155; turned towards

future, 130
division of labour, international, 27, 94
dollar currency, 13

East, as new South, 105–6
East–West relations, 90
ecology *see* environmental issues
Ecuador, 104
education, in USSR, 65
Egypt, 96, 170; marginalization of, 102
11 September attacks, 60
empire of chaos, 1, 17, 121–6, 129
enclosure, global, 38
enlightenment, 18, 19; erasure of, 22
environmental issues, 151, 152, 156, 161
equality, as essential value, 43
ethics, economic and social, 131
euro currency, 13
Euro-Mediterranean dialogue, 151
Europe, 168; investment in USA, 157–8;
    rapprochement with Asia, 149;
    relations with Russia, 66; 'social', 15,
    157
European Court of Justice, 143
European project, 14–17, 148
European Social Forum, 16
European Union (EU), 1, 8–24, 105, 163;
    recovery of, 13
EU–ACP accord, 151
exchange rates, flexible, 109

five monopolies, 3
Fordism, 82; peripheral, 82
Fourth International, 169
fourth world, 92, 150; Arab, 102
France, 16, 132; political culture of, 21
Free Trade Area of the Americas
    (FTAA), 160
French Revolution, 18, 21, 30, 33, 166;
    erasure of, 22

Gandhi, Indira, 77
genocide, 115, 128
geopolitics, 6
Germany, 11, 16, 57; war reparations of, 137
Giscard d'Estaing, Valéry, 22
global campaigns, organization of, 163
globalization, 67, 91, 98; alternative, 1, 5,
    6, 63, 65, 83, 130, 146, 147, 173 (in India,
    79–83); desirable forms of, 5–7;
    economic management of, UN role in,

136–42; humanist response to, 152;
    management of, 107; militarization of,
    140, 164; negotiated, 3; phases of, 2–3
Glorious Revolution (England), 46
Gorbachev, Mikhail, 44, 53, 66
governance, good, 123
green revolution, 71, 74, 75
Group of 7, 123, 131
Group of 8, 112
Group of 20, 104, 160
Group of 77, 86, 115, 148
growth, economic, maximization of, 150
Guevarism, 169, 172
Gulf oil region, 101
Gulf War, 116

Han nation, 44
Hardt, Michael, with Antonio Negri,
    Empire, 153
Harnecker, Marta, 103
Hayek, Friedrich, 35
hegemonic blocs, alternative, 6–7
highly indebted poor countries (HIPCs),
    138
Hindus in India, 72, 76, 79
Hindutva, 78, 111
Hinton, William, 36, 40
human rights: organizations, 72; respect
    for, 127
humanitarian intervention, 133
Hungary, 56

identity, issue of, 154
immigration, constitution of working
    classes, 19
imperialism: collective, 17, 83; nature of,
    2–5; weight of, 167–8
India, 10, 40, 41, 42, 68, 108, 132, 148–9,
    150, 160; as a great power, 69–83;
    colonial inheritance of, 69–72
India–Russia–China bloc, 83
industrial outsourcing, regulation of, 163
industrialization, 4, 39, 52, 87, 88, 94, 96,
    98, 99; in USSR, 53; of periphery, 151
infitah, 102
intellectual property rights, 109, 125
international business law, 124, 125, 142;
    role of UN in, 135
International Court of Justice, 143
International Covenant on Civil and
    Political Rights (ICCPR), 134

International Covenant on Economic, Social and Cultural Rights (ICESCR), 134

International Labour Organization (ILO), 135, 136, 138–9

international law *see* law, international

International Monetary Fund (IMF), 58, 84, 108, 139

intervention: imperialist, 128; in internal affairs of states, 114, 115; military, authorization for, 114 *see also* humanitarian intervention

investment, foreign, regulation of, 109

Iran, 102

Iraq, 102, 108; anti-war movement, 16; invasion of, 62, 129; war against, 61, 131, 132

Islam, 61, 79, 98, 99; political, 83, 99, 101, 111

Islamic movements, 63, 149

Israel, 100, 101–2, 108, 116, 132, 170

Japan, 2, 8–24, 43, 45, 149, 150, 169; investment in USA, 23; prisoner of USA, 23

Japanese model, crisis of, 23

justice: international, UN role in construction of, 126–31, 142–4; social, 152 (UN role in construction of, 126–31)

Karnataka state (India), 83

Kashmir, 77

Keita, Modibo, 86

Kerala, 70

kolkhoz model, 40

Korea, 150

labour unions *see* trade unions

land: access to, 71, 80, 134 (in China, 42; right of, 40, 46, 163); private ownership of, 70–71; privatization of, 159

Latin America, 103–5; attachment to democracy, 159

Latin Americanization, 105

law, international, 112, 122, 126, 127; creation of universal courts, 135; international courts, 142–4; redrafting of, 157; international, UN and, 133–6

League of Nations, 113, 114

Lelio Basso Foundation, 134

Lenin, V.I., 172

liberalism, 76, 77–8, 81, 110, 141

liberty: concept of, 20; in Europe, 21

Libya, blockade of, 102

Lomé–Cotonou accords, 94, 151

'Lula' da Silva, Luiz Inácio, 104, 105, 160

Malaysia, restoration of exchange controls, 109

Maoism, 26–7, 72, 73, 169, 172

Marais, Hein, 98

market, 126, 127; as expression of liberty, 125

Marxism, 35, 73, 167

Mercosur, 160

Mexican Revolution, 103, 166

Mexico, 104

migration: of surplus populations, 53; to cities, 37, 40, 52

military bases: closure of, 163; removal of, 107, 108, 129, 133

mining-based economy of southern Africa, 93

von Mises, Ludwig, 35

mixed economy, 64

Mobutu Sese Seko, 118

modernity: in China, 43; relation to democracy, 42

modernization, 52, 74, 87, 88, 89, 90, 93, 99, 112; of agriculture, 97

Monroe doctrine, 103, 117; extension of, 9–14

Monrovia Group, 86

movement, global, strength of, 160–64

Multilateral Agreement on Investment (MAI), 135, 160

multipolar world, 5, 84, 106; conditions for, 157; construction of, 1, 25, 65, 128, 162 (difficulties of 146–8); in twentieth century, 165–74; UN as part of, 112–45; under Soviet system, 54 *see also* polycentrism

multitude, concept of, 153, 163

Muslims in India, 76, 78

Nahda, 98, 100; failure of, 99

Nasser, Gamal Abdel, 86

nation-building, 170–72

national construction, 91

national discourses, lose legitimacy, 118

national liberation movements, 4, 73, 76,

77, 80, 87, 90, 91, 93, 104, 116, 120, 128, 151, 154
national populism, 98, 99, 101, 104, 113, 115, 170, 171
nationalization, 99; renationalization, 64
natural resources, management of, 140, 156
Naxalite movement (India), 72, 78, 169
Negri, Antonio, 153, 164
neo-conservative revolution, 19
neocolonialism, 94
neoliberalism, 15, 126; avoidance of term, 54–5
networks, 153
Nicaragua, US mining of, 143
Nkrumah, Kwame, 86
Non-Aligned Movement, 45, 77, 81, 86, 101, 104, 109, 115, 134, 148
non-proliferation treaty, 129
North American Free Trade Agreement (NAFTA), 105
North Atlantic Treaty Organization (Nato), 22, 54, 57, 58, 112, 123, 131
North–South relations, 2, 5, 6, 8
Northern Ireland, 154

oil: consumption of, 26; control of resources, 94
oil boom, 102
oil/dollar standard, 13, 158
oligarchy, 56
openness, management of, 27
Opus Dei, 22
Organization of African Unity (OAU), 86
overlap between market, state and society, 119–21

Pakistan, 101
Palestine, 101–2, 108, 116, 132, 170; wall of shame, 143
pan-Arabism, 100
Paris–Berlin–Moscow alliance, 17
patriotic discourse, 62–3
peasant agriculture, 37–8; relation to market agriculture, 39
peasantry, 95, 97, 159, 166; access to land, 80, 134, 152, 160, 163, 174; break-up of, 38, 109; disappearance of, 71; landless, 70, 71; organizations of, 161; revolutionary awareness of, 78; risings of, 72; struggles of, 80, 109

periphery, 92, 96, 103, 116, 120, 167, 168; construction of socialism in, 170–72; industrialization of, 151
pillage economy, 93, 110, 137
Poland, 56
political cultures, clash of, 17–22
polycentrism, 113–14, 116, 118, 123, 129, 155
populist national project, in India, 72–7
poverty: new, 80; reduction of, 74; war on, 117
power, winning of, 163
preventive war, 10, 107, 124
Primakov, Yevgeny, 66
private ownership, 70
productivity of labour, 37
property owners, responsibilities of, regulated, 35–6
public services, management of, 21
Putin, Vladimir, 11, 60

raw materials, falling prices of, 92
Reformation, 19
regional structures, discussion of, 129
regionalism, of Soviet system, 60–61
revolutions: in history, 166–7; reversals of, 45–6
rights: collective, 134; of peoples, 142 (UN and, 133–6)
rural populations, reduction of, 37
Russia, 46, 62, 81, 108, 148–9, 158; alternatives in, 64–8; investment in, 56; member of G7, 61; new forms of capitalism in, 54–64; post-Soviet, 49–68; re-establishment of military power of, 65; trade unions in, 59–60
Russian Federation, dismemberment of, 10
Russian Revolution, 19, 30, 45, 62, 165, 166, 167, 169
Russian–American alliance, 67
Russian–European alliance, 67

Saudi Arabia, 101
Second International, 34, 35
self-sufficiency, rural, 92, 93
separation of powers, 124
shantyization, 38, 40
Sikhs, 77
silk routes, 119, 120
Singh, V.P., 72, 79
slavery, 19

social forums, 164
social movements, 159, 164
socialism, 18, 22, 29, 31, 32, 46, 49, 52, 53,
    62, 73, 89, 90, 91, 126, 147, 149, 163, 165,
    167; actually existing, 54, 74, 113, 116;
    construction of, 170–72; definition of,
    34; fully developed, 34; market-,
    28–39, 157; necessity of democracy, 174;
    transition to, 172–4
socialization, models of, 127
South: advances of, 165; resistance of, 147,
    148, 150; solidarity of, 81, 157, 160
    (rebuilding of, 84–111)
South Africa, 45, 96, 138, 160; as weak
    link, 95–8
sovereignty: conflict with democracy, 128,
    133; national, 116, 118, 127, 130, 132, 140,
    157 (concept of, 133; management of,
    within UN, 112–15); of peoples, 64, 121,
    130, 132, 157 (UN role in construction
    of, 126–31); of states, 112; of US national
    interests, 122–3
Soviet system, 88, 90, 159, 171;
    characteristics of, 49, 50–54; collapse
    of, 55; delinking of, 53–4;
    disintegration of, 58; education in, 55
state: regulatory, 117; intervention by, 89
strikes, in Russia, 59
structural adjustment, 98, 106, 139
struggle, results from, 43
Suharto, Haji Mohamed, 118
Sukarno, Achmad, 86
Syria, 171

Taiwan, 44
Taliban, 118
Tanzania–Zambia railway, 45
taxation, 153, 156; global, 140, 156; of
    consumption, 156; of use of natural
    resources, 140, 155 *see also* Tobin tax
technology, new, absorption of, 41
terror, war on, 67, 123, 124, 133, 149
terrorism, definition of, 133
Third International, 32, 34, 35, 168
Third World, 92; use of term, 87
Tibet, 44
Tobin tax, 139
trade unions, 21, 50, 96, 161; in Russia,
    59–60; in USA, 18, 163
transnational corporations, 4, 17, 107, 139,
    140

triad, 1, 4, 8–24, 26, 56–7, 61, 66, 82, 112,
    121, 139
Tricontinental, 104
Turkey, 102

Uighurs, 44
unemployment, 37
Union of Soviet Socialist Republics
    (USSR), 23, 54, 73, 85, 94, 169, 170;
    break-up of, 29, 52, 55; encirclement
    of, 10, 168; former, 159; relation to Arab
    national movement, 100
United Kingdom, 57
United Nations (UN), 121, 124; and
    international law, 133–6; and rights of
    peoples, 133–6; as guardian of peace,
    129; balance sheet of activity 1945–80,
    115–18; Business Court, 144;
    Declaration of Right to Development,
    134; democratization within, 156;
    founding of, 122; General Assembly,
    117; murder of, 117; political functions
    of, 131–3; proposals for renaissance of,
    131–45; reform of, 112–45, 127–31;
    resolutions, 101, 102, 116; revocation of
    functions of, 112, 122; role of (in
    constructing justice and sovereignty,
    126–31; in disarmament, 133; in
    economic management of
    globalization, 136–42; in international
    business law, 135; in international
    justice, 142–4)
UN Charter, 40, 113, 114–15
UN Conference on Trade and
    Development (UNCTAD), 138–9
UN Security Council, 108, 132, 143
United States of America (USA), 4–5, 65,
    66, 67, 72, 77, 81, 82, 83, 101, 102, 103, 108,
    131, 135, 150, 163; concept of liberty, 20;
    deficit of, 108; hegemonist project of, 1,
    12, 45, 85, 121, 122, 123, 158, 168 (inimical
    to China, 44); in Central Asia and
    Caucasia, 61; interests of, 122–3;
    military project of, 107, 147, 170
    (resistance to, 150, 174; thwarting of,
    148–51); mining of Nicaraguan ports,
    143; project of ruling class, 9–14;
    savings deficit of, 158; trade deficit of,
    12; vulnerability of, 12
US–Israel Middle East project, 101–2,
    151

Universal Declaration of Human Rights, 134
universalism, values of, 126
urbanization, 37, 41, 89, 90, 98

Venezuela, 104, 105, 108
Vienna, Treaty of, 113
Vietnam, 26, 29, 171; revolution in, 166, 168
Vietnam War, 147
voiceless people, giving of voice to, 162

war: ban on, 114; permanence of, 122, 124 *see also* preventive war
war crimes, 115
war on terror *see* terror, war on
water, UN role in management of, 141–2
welfare state, 91, 113
Western Bengal, 70

Westphalia, Treaty of, 113
women: advancement of, 161; demands of, 163
World Bank, 70, 84, 110, 123, 137, 138, 139; agrarian reform programmes, 71
World Forum for Alternatives, 144
world parliament, proposal for, 136, 156
World Social Forum, 162
World Trade Organization (WTO), 57, 58, 65, 104, 109, 124, 125, 135, 139, 142; Dispute Settlement Body, 124; removal of agriculture from agenda of, 159

Yeltsin, Boris, 60
Yemen, South, 172
Yugoslavia, 51, 56, 123, 132; revolution in, 166; under Tito, 154

Zhou Enlai, 40